A GUIDE TO
INTER-RACIAL HARMONY

DEAR WHITE
PEOPLE

IN "POST-RACIAL" AMERICA

JUSTIN SIMIEN

Illustrations by Ian O'Phelan

37INK

ATRIA

New York • London • Toronto • Sydney • New Delhi

ATRIA BOOKS
A Division of Simon & Schuster, Inc.
1230 Avenue of the Americas
New York, NY 10020

First 37 Ink/Atria Books hardcover edition October 2014

37 INK / ATRIA BOOKS and colophon are trademarks of Simon & Schuster, Inc.

For information about special discounts for bulk purchases,
please contact Simon & Schuster Special Sales at 1-866-506-1949 or
business@simonandschuster.com.

The Simon & Schuster Speakers Bureau can bring authors to your
live event. For more information or to book an event contact the
Simon & Schuster Speakers Bureau at 1-866-248-3049 or visit our
website at www.simonspeakers.com.

Illustrations by Ian O'Phelan

Manufactured in the United States of America

10 9 8 7 6 5 4 3 2 1

Library of Congress Cataloging-in-Publication Data
Simien, Justin.
  Dear white people : a guide to inter-racial harmony in "post-racial" America /
Justin Simien. — First 37 Ink/Atria Books hardcover edition.
      pages cm
  1. Whites—United States—Humor. 2. Race awareness—Humor. I. Title.
PN6231.W444S56 2014
  818'.602—dc23   2014034580

ISBN 978-1-4767-9809-7
ISBN 978-1-4767-9810-3 (ebook)

Dedicated to those precious, easily offended few who will courageously take to online comment sections, Twitter, and other semi-anonymous forms of communication to express outrage over this book after having read only its title. Without you I could not sell as many books, and my name would not be as well known.

Contents

[When] Black and Third World people are expected to educate white people as to our humanity . . . the oppressors maintain their position and evade their responsibility for their own actions. There is a constant drain of energy which might be better used in redefining ourselves . . .

—Audre Lorde

Men often hate each other because they fear each other; they fear each other because they don't know each other; they don't know each other because they can not communicate; they can not communicate because they are separated.

—Martin Luther King Jr.,
Stride Toward Freedom: The Montgomery Story, 1958

DEAR WHITE PEOPLE

Start Here

A BRIEF INTRODUCTION

DEAR WHITE PEOPLE

DEAR **WHITE PEOPLE.** It's a catchy title. Catchy but curious, I must concede, and one I imagine you, dear reader, responding to in a number of ways. If you're white, you may walk past this book thinking, *Finally, a manifesto of all the ways I've been marginalizing my ethnic friends!* Or, perhaps, *Fabulous. Another piece of self-deprecating irony I can place on the new coffee table I bought for my trendy loft in a recently gentrified part of town!* If your knee-jerk reaction, however, is something like *This book exemplifies why minorities should not be allowed to have opinions!*, then you may either be a ghost from the Civil War, or the educational system in your county has left you unprepared for the contents of this book.

Another reaction I've encountered while making the film-festival circuit with my movie of the same name comes in the form of *Why should white people be addressed in this manner at all? How are their opinions in any way helpful in fostering a sense of self for people of color?* To this person, I say, You're right, my brother. And thus concludes this book. Black power.

In all seriousness, did you notice what I did at the beginning of this introduction? I just stereotyped you, dear reader. I boxed you into a rigid assumption for the purposes of convenience and humor. For starters, this introduction assumed you were either white or black. This was out of pure ~~laziness~~ convenience. If you're a member of neither race, you're probably in a group being marginalized for some reason or another and, therefore, will hopefully be able to relate. Silver lining!

Second, if you're white, being blatantly stereotyped can be such a foreign or rare experience that it can be taken with grave offense. The Internet eloquently calls this being "butthurt," or deeply offended by something petty. If you're a couple pages in and already butthurt, this is going to be a tough read for you. Your feelings are valid but you may be blind to your own white privilege, in which case I say put this book down, go forth, and enjoy your whiteness! There are so many more organic ice cream flavors to try, and so many employment opportunities to enjoy without suspicion from coworkers who surmise you just got the job because of your race!

More often than not, however, white people laugh at white stereotypes as a bit of nonthreatening humor because most white people are innately aware that opinions about white people from books like *Stuff White People Like* and shows like *Portlandia* pose little threat to their daily lives. Despite this book, white

people will still be able to enjoy Vespa scooters without comment and properly conjugate words without anyone being surprised.

For black folks, being stereotyped is nothing new, but it typically can have a very real impact on their daily lives, even when it comes in the form of well-meaning gestures and questions from their white friends or colleagues like, "As a Black Person, why do you think people talk back to the screen in movies?" These are called "microaggressions." It's not lynch-mob racism, but being spoken to or even treated in a kind way because of an assumption about your race by a member of a race that on the whole has cultural, political, and economic control can feel unsettling.

The title *Dear White People* represents the exasperating, sometimes funny, sometimes enraging process of navigating race in the so-called post-Obama age. An age where racism remains alive and well despite the assumption of far too many people that racism ended around 2008 with Obama's election. While it's true the book is partly organized by a list of things white people should know on behalf of black people,[1] it's actually meant to provoke a discussion among all people about race and identity as understood from a black perspective. If you're willing to laugh at yourself a little and admit that race in America can still be a minefield of miscommunication whether you're black, white, or

---

[1] I was voted this year's spokesperson at the last Congressional Black Caucus Legislative Conference. That's how the Congressional Black Caucus works, right?

other, you will enjoy this book! I suppose I could've saved us both the trouble of this introduction and just called my book something else. But honestly, if I had titled it something along the lines of *Ruminations on Race: Essays on Identity from an African American Perspective,* which, frankly, it is, then we both would have fallen asleep. Just now. And as I've discovered in recent months, falling asleep while writing is, surprisingly, not an effective method for finishing a book.

To be fair, the primary reason behind calling my book *Dear White People* is because without having made the aforementioned movie of the same title, I would not have gotten this gig. The film involves a character whose college radio show lambasts her white classmates for unintended racism, but the film is not about white people at all. Instead, the "black experience" of four students at an Ivy League college is the primary focus of the film. It's cool. You should check it out, or whatever.

This book operates much like the movie. Though it may come in the form of an address to white people at large, it's really about black people and, by proxy, members of other marginalized cultures who may have similar feelings and experiences. And while I'm aware of the irony and confusion inherent in addressing a book to white people that primarily deals with America as seen from the margins, i.e., the American experience from a black point of view, here's the thing: Name recognition + controversy =

a new yacht. And by "yacht," I of course mean an important cultural discussion.[2]

Now that we live in a "post-racial" America—thanks to the election of President Obama and the success of whichever Beyoncé album has been surreptitiously released by the time of this publication—it seems people of all races are starting to figure out how to hang out together. And with the kind of casual intermingling of the races once envisioned by Dr. Martin Luther King Jr. and the casting director of the original season of the *Mighty Morphin Power Rangers,* many people of all persuasions are discovering that not only does "post-racism" mean "denial of racism," it also means that there is a multitude of microaggressions between mainstream and marginalized cultures brewing that go unexpressed.

I've noticed that people typically want to discuss race in America only if it comes in the form of irony or controversy, or a civil rights/slavery-era film released during awards season. So, contrirony it is! I'd rather you pick up the book and argue over it than have you add it to your mental queue of things you *should* read as you pick up a copy of *Gone Girl,* which, to be honest, you really should have read by now.

Still confused, outraged, or otherwise unconvinced about this humble author's choice of title? Here is a list of other books with similarly misleading titles:

---

[2] Obviously. The real money in writing a book is getting someone to make a movie based on it and, frankly, it's too late for that.

BOOK TITLE	YOU THINK IT'S ABOUT	IT'S ACTUALLY ABOUT
The Jungle by Upton Sinclair	A thrilling adventure that takes place in the tropics.	A depiction of the personal rights abuses of the immigrant labor force in Chicago during the early twentieth century. Also, your meat may contain E. coli.
1984 by George Orwell	The future (at the time of publication) or the past (at the time of now).	~~Present day America.~~ A fictional world where a totalitarian government manipulates its citizens through official deception, surveillance, and media propaganda.
To Kill a Mockingbird by Harper Lee	An anti-bird revenge fantasy and/or a *Hunger Games* sequel.	The trial of a black man who is wrongly accused of raping a white woman in a small racist town that somehow is not in Florida.
The Circle by Dave Eggers	Geometry	The dangers of sharing too much on social media. #whoops #unsubscribe #thankgodfortheeditbutton

See? Creating controversial work with misleading titles is nothing new. But truthfully, what I've found while playing the film to audiences of all races across the country is that *most* people are neither confused nor shocked by the title. The most common reaction is a simple chuckle of recognition. With either a "Yeah, I've

used that phrase" or a "Yeah, I probably said something that merited someone directing that phrase toward me."

So to answer the real question at hand—Is this book for you?—try answering the following:

1. Are you a white person seeking to make your nonwhite friends feel more comfortable in your presence?
2. Are you looking for a humorous outlet for your budding annoyance with the feeling of being marginalized by people's assumptions about you?
3. Are you in an interracial relationship and want an easy, passive-aggressive way to bring your white partner up to speed on what never to do or say?
4. Are you looking to create a more inclusive workspace for your employees?
5. Are you looking for items to decorate your office or apartment and let people know it's cool; you're cool?
6. Do you have the asking price for this book?

If you answered yes to any or none of the above questions, this book is for you. Purchase and read on!

BLACK MYTH BUSTERS

Post-Racism

The idea that America has somehow become "post-racial" remains popular thanks to President Barack Obama's election/re-election as well as Neil deGrasse Tyson replacing Stephen Hawking as the guy who comes up when you google "smart sciencey man" while stoned. It's also a popular idea among people who fancy themselves colorblind and therefore absolved from having a conversation about racism.

Unfortunately, "post-racism" is also a myth, like unicorns and black people who survive until the end of a horror movie. We still live in a country where a person of color is at a major disadvantage to their white peers because of privileges and opportunities denied to them. Morgan Freeman playing the president and God in popular films wasn't enough to save Barack Obama from literally being asked by other people in power to "go back to Africa." Just as Barack Obama becoming the first black president doesn't instantly solve the problem of income, health, and housing disparities based on race. Nor has it stopped unarmed black teenagers from being shot by overzealous police officers and suspicious white citizens "standing their ground."

The idea of "post-racism," just like that of "reverse racism," is really just a coded way of denying the existence of actual racism. And denying the existence of actual racism is really just another form of (you guessed it) *racism*. Also, if you've been playing the drinking game Take a Shot Every Time You See the Word "Racism," you will probably develop liver disease over the course of reading this book. Racism.

HANDS OFF

REPELS THE CURIOUS TOUCH OF WHITE FINGERS

REALLY?
NO
SERIOUSLY?

This goes for MEN & WOMEN!

Please Stop Touching My Hair

OR, ON BEING MISTAKEN FOR A PETTING ZOO

SOMEHOW, despite warnings from most black comedians and that reflexive deer-in-the-headlights look that most black people adopt when asked about it, black hair continues to be a black hole for white people's fingers.

At a screening of my film *Dear White People*, a distraught older white woman came up to me with tears in her eyes. She assured me that her desire to touch the hair of her friends came from a place of love. It was only after I gently removed her trembling hands from the back of my scalp, told her it was "just a movie," and hid behind a display for *Transformers: Age of Extinction* that I came up with what would have been a far more effective response. I should have told her that her best intentions notwithstanding, if she'd only bothered to ask her black friends if they liked being fondled by anyone other than their lover, she'd understand what an imposition it was.

The Spectacle of Natural Hair

Admittedly, there are few things as beguiling as natural hairstyles in *all* their diversity. However, thanks to the prevalence of Eurocentric beauty standards and the lasting influence of Lil' Kim, it's rare to see even a dreadlock in mainstream media. Unless one has actual black friends it's unlikely a white person will encounter a frohawk, a lobster roll, and/or a snail bun.[3] These concoctions of kinky and curly can be as stunning as any work of art, but I'd urge anyone to refrain from showing their appreciation by probing with their fingers.

For one, there are a number of mysterious hidden energies at play keeping that chunky crown twist together. Whether it's shea butter, styling spray, or the Holy Spirit, the integrity of many a hairdo relies on being kept safe from white finger resin. Logistics of keeping a hairdo intact aside, science[4] tells us that even casual touch can communicate startling degrees of social dominance and intimacy between two people. Outside of accepted codes of casual physical contact such as handshaking and fake hugging between celebrities on red carpets, too much touching can feel threatening to the recipient. Even though one might be filled with awe at the sight of a real-life twisted upknot, simmer. Consider what would happen if you did that at the Museum of Modern Art and the subject of your fascination was a Picasso. Simply by *asking* to touch the art, you would get confused and irritated looks from the security guards. Appreciation must come hand in hand with restricted use of said hands.

---

[3] Google them. They're unbelievable.

[4] I.e., cursory Google search.

The "How Does She Do It?" Effect

Another source of curiosity when it comes to black hair is its uncanny ability to shape-shift. A white coworker might wonder with admiration, no less, how a black woman can come to work with a Halle Berry–style pixie cut one day and a shoulder-length blow-out the next. "How does she do it?" this hypothetical white coworker might say sotto voce. And while that's a fair question, using your fingers to find the answer will only ensure that Sheryl[5] in accounting will stop inviting you to lunch.

In order to prevent well-meaning white hands from wandering into the headspace of secretly outraged black people, I will outline here exactly how "Sheryl" and every black woman does it.

The truth is, black women are magic. All of them. Not just Angela Bassett in *American Horror Story: Coven.* The ability to transform curly hair into straight hair and brown into blond begins to manifest around age thirteen for most black girls. The no-lye relaxer product Just for Me! that's marketed to children is really just a cover. Inside every box is an at-home study kit designed to teach young black girls how to control and manifest their

---

[5] If your first thought is, *Why didn't the author decide to name this hypothetical black woman Shaniqua or Aquanetta to make it clear it was the black coworker as opposed to using a footnote,* you are a racist. Read this book five times and watch Spike Lee's *Malcolm X* immediately.

burgeoning hair-shape-shifting abilities as they become women. It's the black female version of what happens in *Harry Potter* when one of those sweet white children becomes old enough to learn to be a wizard.

It's not a great idea to ask a black person any direct questions about the aforementioned magic, as, generally, we are not allowed to speak on its origin. The consequences can be fatal, and I am risking everything I have to give you this information. While it may come at a cost to me and my family, I wanted *you* to know. The coexistence of the races is that important to me.

I know some of you must be thinking, *This is a preposterous and thinly veiled attempt to obscure the use of relaxers, weaves, and lace fronts.* Trust me on this one: Unless she tells you otherwise herself, every black woman's hair, though it may change dramatically from day to day in ways that defy nature, is absolutely her God-given, though possibly magically altered, hair. White people: Do not broach this topic. It doesn't matter that you've seen the Chris Rock documentary *Good Hair.* Like your favorite movie *Frozen* suggests, "Let It Go."

Not Getting Slapped

For some black people, being asked for permission to have their hair touched or, worse yet, having it touched by surprise elicits a viscerally negative reaction. We can't help it. According to the theories of Carl Jung, which I vaguely remember skimming on Wikipedia, all of us have powerful genetic memories going back to our ancestors. Do not be surprised if a black person responds to a request to touch their hair by defiantly yelling out, "I AM KUNTA KINTE!" They are subconsciously recalling that scene in *Roots* when Geordi from *Star Trek* is being poked and prodded by a slave trader. Thus is the nature of genetic memory, probably.

Even if images from made-for-TV slavery stories aren't the first things that come to mind for the person on the receiving end of all of this curiosity, the feeling of being on display at, say, a petting zoo isn't one anyone would want to feel at work, home, or play. Adding adorable phrases around the request doesn't help either. Whether you're saying, "Wow, that's beautiful; may I?"; "Your little naps are so cute!"; or "Lower yo' head, boy, so Massa can inspect you," it all comes across, more or less, in the same way.

There are, of course, some notable exceptions to this rule. In intimate relationships, for instance, it is natural and, in many cases, desirable for a white partner to run his or her fingers through and even pull a lover's hair, whether it's natural, short, cropped, or straightened via magic.

The ultimate expression of this is when a black person asks a white partner to grease his or her scalp. If you're on the receiving end of this request, try to fight the confusion that you will inevitably feel and recognize this request as the sacred honor that it is. You've reached the blackest state possible for any white person to reach. Much like enlightenment, it is a rare and oftentimes fleeting state of being. Savor it. And pray you can pull up that Mars Blackmon scene from *She's Gotta Have It* on your mobile phone for instructions as you pretend to go to the restroom and look for a comb and some pomade.

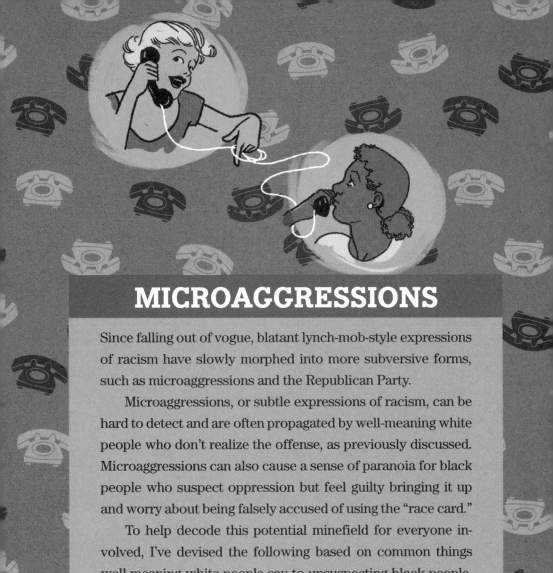

MICROAGGRESSIONS

Since falling out of vogue, blatant lynch-mob-style expressions of racism have slowly morphed into more subversive forms, such as microaggressions and the Republican Party.

Microaggressions, or subtle expressions of racism, can be hard to detect and are often propagated by well-meaning white people who don't realize the offense, as previously discussed. Microaggressions can also cause a sense of paranoia for black people who suspect oppression but feel guilty bringing it up and worry about being falsely accused of using the "race card."

To help decode this potential minefield for everyone involved, I've devised the following based on common things well-meaning white people say to unsuspecting black people. Using the translation chart on pages 23–25, white people can hopefully remove the thorn of racial oppression from their everyday small talk!

Microaggression Translation Chart

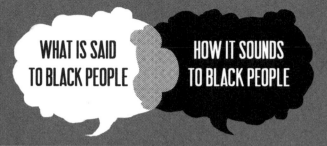

WHAT IS SAID TO BLACK PEOPLE

HOW IT SOUNDS TO BLACK PEOPLE

From a White Person Older Than You		
"Wow, you're so incredibly well spoken!"	**=**	"My God, a negro that has command over basic English? How novel!"
From a Store Clerk		
"You know, those are really expensive . . ."	**=**	"I'm assuming you have no money and am nervous you're going to rob me."
From a Well-Meaning Friend		
"You look just like Beyoncé."	**=**	"You and Beyoncé are the only black women I can think of at the moment."
From a Douchebag Friend		
"Yeah, but you're not *black* black."	**=**	"Since all of your positive qualities are not ones I know to be affiliated with your race, I refuse to acknowledge the fact that you're black."

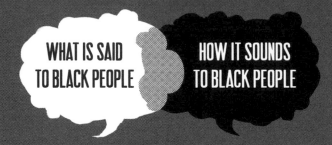

WHAT IS SAID TO BLACK PEOPLE

HOW IT SOUNDS TO BLACK PEOPLE

From a New Coworker		
"Wow, so how did you get this job?"	=	"You got this job unfairly because of Affirmative Action, right?"

From a History Teacher		
"*You're* black, what do you think?"	=	"You have the same thoughts, experiences, and feelings as every member of your race, right? Please represent them!"

From a Potential Employer Not Calling		
" . . . "	=	"You may have had a great résumé, but we stopped at your ethnic-sounding name."

From a Armchair Sociologist		
"Black people can be racist too."	=	"The oppression you perceive in your daily life is a delusion."

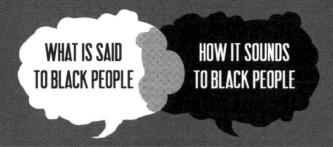

WHAT IS SAID TO BLACK PEOPLE

HOW IT SOUNDS TO BLACK PEOPLE

From a Potential Date		
"I'm really into black guys like you."	=	"You are not a person to me, but merely the fulfillment of a race-based fetish fantasy I have."

From a Associate or Colleague		
"This is going to sound kind of racist, but . . ."	=	"This is absolutely going to be racist, but you can't get mad, okay?"

From a Person You Just Met Who Doesn't Normally Talk Like That		
"What's up, ma brutha?"	=	"If I talk to you this way, you might not shoot me."

From a Person You Just Met Who Is Trying to Make Conversation		
"You know what movie I love? *Precious.*"	=	"Since you're black, I'm assuming you can relate to being poor, overweight, and a victim of repeated child abuse."

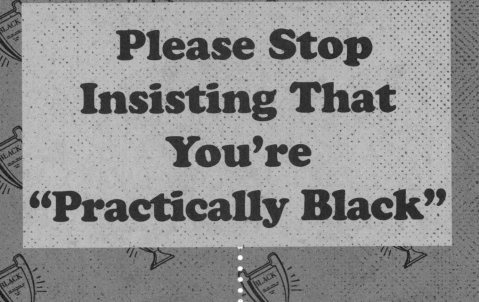

Please Stop Insisting That You're "Practically Black"

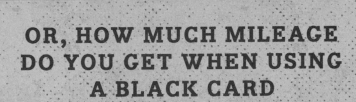

OR, HOW MUCH MILEAGE DO YOU GET WHEN USING A BLACK CARD

Ghetto

Contrary to popular belief,
not all black people are Straight Out of Compton,
though we are each fabulous in our own way,
ghetto or otherwise.

WHETHER IT'S to complain that racism affects them too in the *Dear White People* YouTube comment sections, or to calm anxiety over being at a Wiz Khalifa concert, for some white people being "practically black" is an aspiration. To the white folks to whom this applies, there are a few things about this that are unsettling to your black friends. Black people instinctively know, having had the benefit of being black for some time, that not only is race not a choice, but it's also difficult to define. What exactly makes you "practically black"? A love of hip-hop? A preference for fried chicken? If you think these things combined with your addiction to *The Real Housewives of Atlanta* make you "practically black," the black experience in general might be lost on you.

The other question one should consider when aspiring to blackness is: What exactly does being practically black get you? Hopefully, your black friends are already up for hanging out with you and treating you like an equal, regardless of your race or ethnicity. If not, you have terrible friends. Also, does your being "practically black" bring with it any negative side effects? For example, are police officers aware of your "near-blackness" when deciding whether to pull you over when they spot a broken taillight? How about potential employers who filter out ethnic names before calling you in for an interview? Do you carry the weight of knowing that because of the way people perceive you, you're subjugated to a barrage of assumptions when meeting new people, shopping, or looking for Pop-Tarts under the gaze of suspicious gas station employees?

To be fair, this idea that a white person can be black has its cultural precedence. Michael Rapaport, Bill Clinton, and Eminem come to mind. Some black folks have decided that they, and a few select others, do get the benefits of being identified as black in parts of the world. Making a fantastic documentary on A Tribe Called Quest or playing the saxophone on the original *Arsenio Hall Show* somehow just makes it an easier pill for black folks to swallow. But by and large, getting that Honorary Black Card takes a level of persistence and commitment to the plight and varied experiences of being black in this country that most people aren't prepared to make. I'm barely prepared to make that commitment to myself! But then again, I have no choice. And maybe that's really the defining difference. Black people don't really have much say in the matter of being black.

This is partly what's so soul-shattering about a white person claiming they are "blacker" than an actual black person whose interests lay outside of the stereotypes imposed on black people. If you're white but grew up in Bed-Stuy, majored in African American

Studies, married a black person, and guest DJ for Hip-Hop Saturday at a local nightclub, you will still never be as black as the nerdy black guy in your office who plays Dungeons & Dragons and skateboards in his free time. For one, do you know how awkward it is being the one black guy in a Dungeons & Dragons tournament?[6] And, two, the black experience is one that comes from the experience of being black, not from slipping into cultural concepts like one would a brand-new jacket. So while a white person can never become black (and, yes, I've made a conscious decision to forget the movie *Soul Man* ever happened), it is possible, with persistence and dedication, to receive an Honorary Black Card. It may be the civil union of race experiences, but it's the best we can do. When applying for yours, it is helpful to avoid the following common mistakes.

Being Black in a Past Life

Yeah, this one doesn't get you anywhere. While some black folks will be willing to accept that 1) reincarnation is real and 2) you were black in your past life, the odds are much more likely that you just really enjoy singing along to "How Will I Know" in the car. Worse still, you may simply have condensed the whole of the black experience down to a couple of stereotypes you identify with, like

---

[6] This is not coming from personal experience. I don't have the balls for the kind of cultural toggling required to be a black Dungeons & Dragons fan.

being outspoken or having an ample behind and, having no other way to process these similarities, conclude they are evidence of your past life.

The other possibility is that you were black in a past life, and the experience was so terrible that you opted to come back as white, which would make you a race traitor. Or that you thought by coming back as a white person who used to be black you could somehow help people who are black in this life, like Brad Pitt's character, Bass, in *12 Years a Slave*. This means you have some strange karmic messiah complex. In any case, this is just a losing argument.

Hip-Hop Is Not Synonymous with Black

Hip-hop started out in the black community, no doubt about it. And even with the success of white acts such as the Beastie Boys, Eminem, and Macklemore, it still remains fueled primarily by black artists. Yes, Nicki Minaj counts as a black artist! How dare you. For portions of white America, hip-hop is the only lens through which black culture is seen. This is troubling thanks to shows such as *Love & Hip Hop,* with its weave-snatching and splashing-drinks-in-the-face antics. But also because while hip-hop is certainly a part of many black people's lives, it's not always a defining part, if a part at all. Associating gold chains, champagne-soaked ~~strippers~~

models, and a propensity for drug cocktails with "being black" is problematic for a host of reasons. One, that's really only Top 40 hip-hop. Two, ain't nobody got that kind of scratch to be wasting good champagne on a ~~big booty ho~~ model. Oh, and it's a lazy, offensive stereotype.

It probably won't even make sense in a couple of years. You see, given enough time, every form of music black people invent is eventually Columbused[7] by white people. R&B is basically just code for Justin Timberlake and Robin Thicke now. Disco is now called "dance music." Rock and roll is now "alternative." In the future, the black hip-hop artist will likely be an anomaly. Like Darius Rucker. The day when even rap will be completely Columbused is fast approaching. You'll eventually need a broader definition of black people, so might as well start now!

Other Options

There are a few other things one can do to earn an Honorary Black Card, but none of them are guarantees. Being an African American Studies minor, for instance. This one is a double-edged sword. There's a thin line between enlightening and annoying your black friends by unceremoniously bringing up topics on welfare statistics

---

[7] See p. 96.

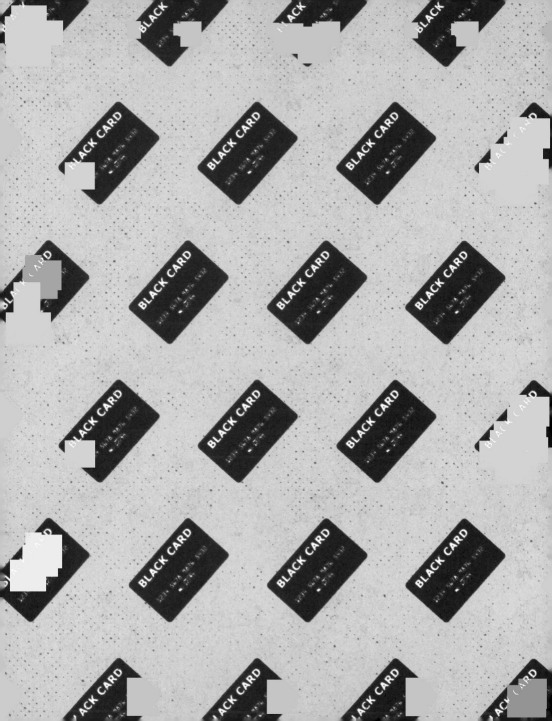

and obscure civil rights leaders. However, being an African American Studies minor and never touting this with your black friends, all the while existing comfortably beside them without touching anyone's hair or asking off-putting questions? That might get you a card.

You could also try dating a black person, though this will require a long-term commitment. A white person in an interracial relationship, toggling between mostly white and mostly black worlds, probably has the best secondhand version of the black experience, after all. After years of romantic association with a black person, you will learn exactly what it's like wading through a sea of presumptions and prejudices from members of both races. Congrats, an Honorary Black Card may be headed your way!

Most of the white people in the Honorary Black Hall of Fame tend to be people who weren't necessarily looking for the distinction. There was no desire to appropriate a race or a culture to bolster their image; they were just following their interests and passions wherever they took them. Relax. Accept your whiteness. Odds are, most black people will be willing to as well.

THE N-WORD

A Decision Tree

Nothing has stirred up the fervent kind of black-white debate that the N-Word has. And by the N-Word, I of course mean "nepotism." Wait, sorry, that was a typo. Of course, I mean "nigga." You'll note the use of the "a" at the end of the word. And what a difference a well-placed "a" can make! The "a" taking the place of the "er" in the word "nigger" somehow elevated a hateful derogatory word used to oppress black people and turned it into a euphemism much enjoyed by rappers and Quentin Tarantino. Yes, *nigga* seems to be the glue by which a Tarantino screenplay involving black people is held together, which begs the question *Is it ever okay for a white person to use it?* It seems that restricting white people's right to say the word has had the same effect as prohibition did on liquor. Whether at a Jay-Z concert, or joking with their good black friends who "know what's up," hearing a young white person say the N-Word is rather common. So what are the ground rules? By using the "Can I Say the N-Word?" Decision Tree, you can discover for yourself!

CAN I SAY THE N-WORD?

ARE YOU BLACK?

ARE YOU CURRENTLY HAVING A CONVERSATION WITH OPRAH WINFREY?

— YES →

ACTUALLY BI-RACIAL

PARTIALLY

IMAGINARY

ARE YOU QUOTING RAP LYRICS?

— NO —

— YES —

NO

ARE YOU SAYING IT ALONG WITH OTHER BLACK PEOPLE?

— YES —

GO FOR IT!

NO

YES

LIKE IN A "PAST LIFE," PARTIALLY, OR LIKE ONE OF YOUR PARENTS?

MAYBE, BUT BE PREPARED TO RUN.

NO

NO

ARE YOU AT A KKK RALLY?

— NO —

YES

NOT TODAY, SON!

Are you giving a dissertation on the eytmological root of the word?

— NO —

NO

IN ORDER TO DISCOURAGE ITS USE?

— YES —

YES

YES

BLACK MYTH BUSTERS
Welfare

Calling out the supposed "abuse" of welfare by blacks and other people of color is a time-honored tactic for distracting the general public from actual national issues. It also taps into latent, subconscious racism, which is what right-wing politicians would call a "win-win." The truth, however, is that by the end of the twentieth century there were fewer blacks enrolled in U.S. welfare programs than whites. In fact, in 2012 a blog from the *New York Times*[8] reported that while 22 percent of the poor are African Americans and are receiving 14 percent of government benefits, white non-Hispanics make up 42 percent of the poor and receive 69 percent of government benefits.

By the end of the last century, welfare accounted for just over 2 percent of the U.S. federal budget, whereas defense spending accounted for 24 percent. Between bank bailouts and contracts to meet the demands of war efforts in other countries, white people are, on the whole, the primary beneficiaries of government handouts in this country.

In conclusion, the real welfare queens are not black women living in Chicago with a gang of kids. More than likely it's actually a white former bank CEO in an apartment overlooking Central Park, possibly swimming in a pool of gold coins like Scrooge McDuck, or whatever it is evil rich people are into these days.

---

[8] From "Who Benefits From the Safety Net" by Binyamin Appelbaum and Robert Gebeloff for nytimes.com; http://nyti.ms/1jG4lBk.

Reality TV Is the New Blackface

OR, FROM MAMMY TO HOUSEWIFE

ONCE UPON A TIME, white America's primary introduction to black people came in the form of the Minstrel Show. Stock characters, often played by white people, such as the Mammy, Zip Coon, and, of course, Jim Crow popularized through entertainment the idea that black people were lazy, ignorant, overly emotional, unsophisticated, and intellectually bereft. These ideas about black people are still being popularized today in entertainment thanks to white television executives (and, to be fair, some black ones too). Though the catchphrases have gone from "Who dat?" to "Who gon' check me, boo?," reality TV has kept the stereotypes tap-dancing along and made them more popular than ever!

Did you know that text-message exchanges between millennials today are comprised almost entirely of animated GIFs of NeNe Leakes rolling her eyes and Omarosa throwing shade? Yes, the stereotype of the "black bitch" has become its own language for some, thanks to a combination of basic cable television programming and general illiteracy among said millennials. To be honest, this entire book has been translated for me from an original manuscript constructed mostly with GIFs of Prince winking and that lemur with the super-big eyes.

What's particularly disturbing about this, implications of our collapsing educational system notwithstanding, is that stereotypes from the slack-jawed, no-good black male to the sexually promiscuous, foul-mouthed black woman are so ubiquitous, groups of people in the country assume that this is how all black people really behave. Now the confused, shuffling Mammies and flamboyant, vapid Zip Coons of yesteryear are actually real people, competing for Donald Trump's affection and/or that of each other's man. I use the term "real people" loosely. The truth is that people in reality shows are cast, crafted, and coached by a staff of executives and writers to attract the biggest audience possible. They are filmed and then re-filmed, with bits of dialogue added to attain maximum absurdity. They are then edited and beamed to millions, validating the worst stereotypes of black folks for people whose contact with actual black people is limited. And boy, are they fun!

Of course, the same thing is happening with Italians from Jersey, Shahs that live on Sunset, women in general, white people hunting for gator in the swamp, and any other group of people willing to cash in on the stereotypes of their niche culture. The thing is, with black folks in particular, the spectrum of representation is already terribly limited. The Olivia Pope character on *Scandal* simply cannot wash away the impressions of all the shucking and jiving happening between black people on reality TV. And no, Honey Boo Boo does not make up for it. I imagine this problem is even worse for Persians. Or swamp dwellers, for that matter. But I leave it to them to write their own books.

The worst part about this whole thing? I watch it. And so do my black friends! *The Real Housewives of Atlanta*! I was in the front row for Kandi's wedding! I watched every spin-off they made for *Flavor of Love*'s "New York," Tiffany Pollard. *I Love New York*? Me too! *New*

York Goes to Work—sign me up for overtime! I am part of the problem. This chapter is my penance! Of course I feel bad about it, but deep down I know it's all fake. Like professional wrestling. There are a lot of people out there, though, who don't know it's not real. Somehow bad improv and staged fighting shot with minimal production value got called "reality" before becoming an American phenomenon.

Talk and televised court shows are also partly to blame for this. America's obsession with paternity tests between people who should not be allowed to procreate for any reason regardless of their race reached a fever pitch in the '90s and early 2000s before becoming a precursor for the kinds of reality TV we know and love today. And most of the men sweating out the revelation of the results, ready to cuss their ex-girlfriends out for putting them on the spot or run offstage and evade responsibility, were black men. Babies having babies (not to mention going on national television to prove whose babies they were), indeed.

Stereotypes are dangerous, because sometimes they're true. And it's easy to focus on some examples of behavior and draw assumptions about an entire group. This is an issue not only because it's often the way some white people learn about black people, but also because it's the way some black people learn about themselves. Entire generations of young black girls are now growing up modeling their lives after vicious stereotypes in the hopes that they can take a shortcut to fame by being picked for *Bad Girls Club* or by mounting a ridiculous lawsuit on *Judge Judy*.

One of the fun things, I assume, about being white is that there are so many varying examples of behavior attributed to white people in the media. It must be a bit easier to walk through life without dodging as many presumptions. Sure, there are white people who appear in their share of trashy television, but that accounts for just a percentage of the overall, mostly positive, images of white folks in the media. For black folks the variety of images adds up to a pretty short stack. Partly because television executives are ~~checking Facebook~~ super busy and are ~~afraid of losing their jobs~~ under a lot of pressure. While there may be a desire to expand the representation of the African diaspora, deep in the heart of this hypothetical TV exec, it's a lot easier just to go with another show about a semi-famous rapper who has a bevy of loud and crazy girlfriends. Or a house filled with alcoholics, the alcohol that's slowly killing them, and a couple of black women who are either "not there to make friends" or who will "cut a bitch."

Whether the focus is housewives or hoarders, we have blissfully confused entertainment for information. Shaky zooms and bad lighting be damned, odds are if it's on TV, whether in the form of news or reality, its primary purpose is to get you to watch long enough to be marketed laundry detergent and soda, not necessarily to paint a wholly accurate picture. With that in mind, here is a guide that will help you decode the ways in which old minstrel characters have evolved into popular reality TV go-to archetypes. We both know you can't stop watching, but at least now you will know why you feel so bad about it!

Guide to Minstrelsy in Reality TV

SAMBO

The simple, hapless, childlike, and lazy slave. Sometimes he was fat and jolly, sometimes portrayed as an actual child, but always utterly dependent on white people to save him, like his ever understanding Massa!

=

"HOOD" CELEBRITY

The simple, charming, vaguely intoxicated trouble-maker, whose charm and general harmlessness get him out of trouble. Sometimes a C-list hip-hop star or wannabe hustler, this character's hap-lessness is often both frustrat-ing to those in his real life and funny to the audience.

MAMMY

An obese, matriarchal figure who took care of white people's children with tenderness while raising hell in her own home and dominating her husband. Also the basis for the design of a popular line of pancake syrup bottles.

=

HOUSEWIFE

A woman, typically with a great deal of makeup, married to a hardly seen but usually rich man. She tends to have a penchant for wigs and Spanx, sassily dominates her husband and children, and strives to impress influential white people in society.

MANDINGO A brutish, savage black male, whose intellect, ambitions, interests, dreams, and fears all served to feed his ravenous sexual appetite. While that may read like the plot of a Zane novel, back in the day this was seen as very bad.	**=**	**THE PLAYER** Sometimes he's the husband of an aforementioned House-wife or friendly with a main character, but he's always hus-tling, conniving, and scheming to sleep with women, cheat on his significant other, and make it rain at strip clubs.
SAPPHIRE While usually a matriarch like the Mammy, the Sapphire's dominant characteristics are her headstrong, bossy, verbally abusive ways. Ever cantan-kerous and independent, she was never anywhere to "make friends."	**=**	**THE BITCH** While sometimes a Housewife, The Bitch is particularly popular in competition-based reality shows. She's domineering, ar-rogant, mean, and headstrong. If she's intelligent, that usually comes into play to berate others and defend her turf. She's also not here to "make friends."
JEZEBEL Created in a kind of cultural wet dream to absolve white men of their guilt over finding black women attractive, the Jezebel was a grand seduc-tress. She had an insatiable sexual appetite and thrived on being "bad."	**=**	**THE CRAZY BITCH** Usually a version of The Bitch but often single and with the added benefit of a drinking problem or mental disorder. The Crazy Bitch will usually do anything to steal someone's man or throw a drink in some-one's face. The Crazy Bitch and The Bitch tend to fight the most fervently over ~~camera-time~~ things important to them.

ZIP COON

Also sometimes called Jim Crow, Zip Coon was a shuffling, wisecracking buffoon whose attempts to adopt the sophistication and style of white culture always resulted in failure. This was the most popular of caricatures used in Minstrelsy partly because while he had the talent it took to be more than a slave, he was proof of the ultimate inferiority of the negro.

=

THE GAY PET

Usually the subservient, black gay sidekick, he is responsible for teaching The Crazy Bitch how to use new and exciting slang from the black gay underground or validating a Housewife's choice of wig. The Gay Pet's cultural ambitions are often paired with a lack of taste. He is wildly entertaining thanks to his wit, but is ultimately nonthreatening and has limited power. Sometimes the Gay Pet is put in his place through an altercation with The Player or one of The Bitches.

THE MAGICAL NEGRO

The patient and wise, usually mentally or physically disabled black man whose role in life was to come to the aid of a white hero with advice or actual magic. While a more recent development, The Magical Negro had its roots in the ever-pleasing Sambo character, with a mythic relationship to nature that had echoes of the animal-like Mandingo.

=

THE BLACK EXPERT

The wise and well-meaning, sometimes but not always well-spoken authority on black people, usually brought on a news program or morning talk show to give the black insight into whatever event is being discussed. They can also be a recurring character in an otherwise white reality show, there to bestow black wisdom so as to aid well-meaning white people.

SHOULD YOU WEAR BLACKFACE?

A Decision Tree

So . . . somehow, blackface is still a thing. Painting one's face in charcoal-black makeup, highlighting it with giant red or white lips, and portraying dangerous and offensive stereotypes for paying audiences was once America's greatest national pastime. Thanks to reality TV, it still is. Without the charcoal-black makeup, of course. Said makeup would make it blatantly racist and it would therefore be difficult to convince corporations to consider placing ads in certain lucrative time slots.

But occasionally, despite being mired in the backlash over what is widely perceived as bigotry, white people seem fascinated by trotting out the old tradition. Whether it's to "celebrate" their favorite television show characters at a Halloween party or to "honor" Black History Month, every year white people, be they celebrities or misguided college students, get in trouble for wearing blackface and promoting it on their Instagram accounts.

The situation is made murky by satirical uses of blackface in recent years. Why is it acceptable for Robert Downey Jr. to don blackface in *Tropic Thunder*, for instance, but Julianne Hough is called on the carpet for dressing as her favorite character, Crazy Eyes, from *Orange Is the New Black*? Here to help is a comprehensive decision tree suitable for any and all situations that might have you wondering if it's okay to wear blackface.

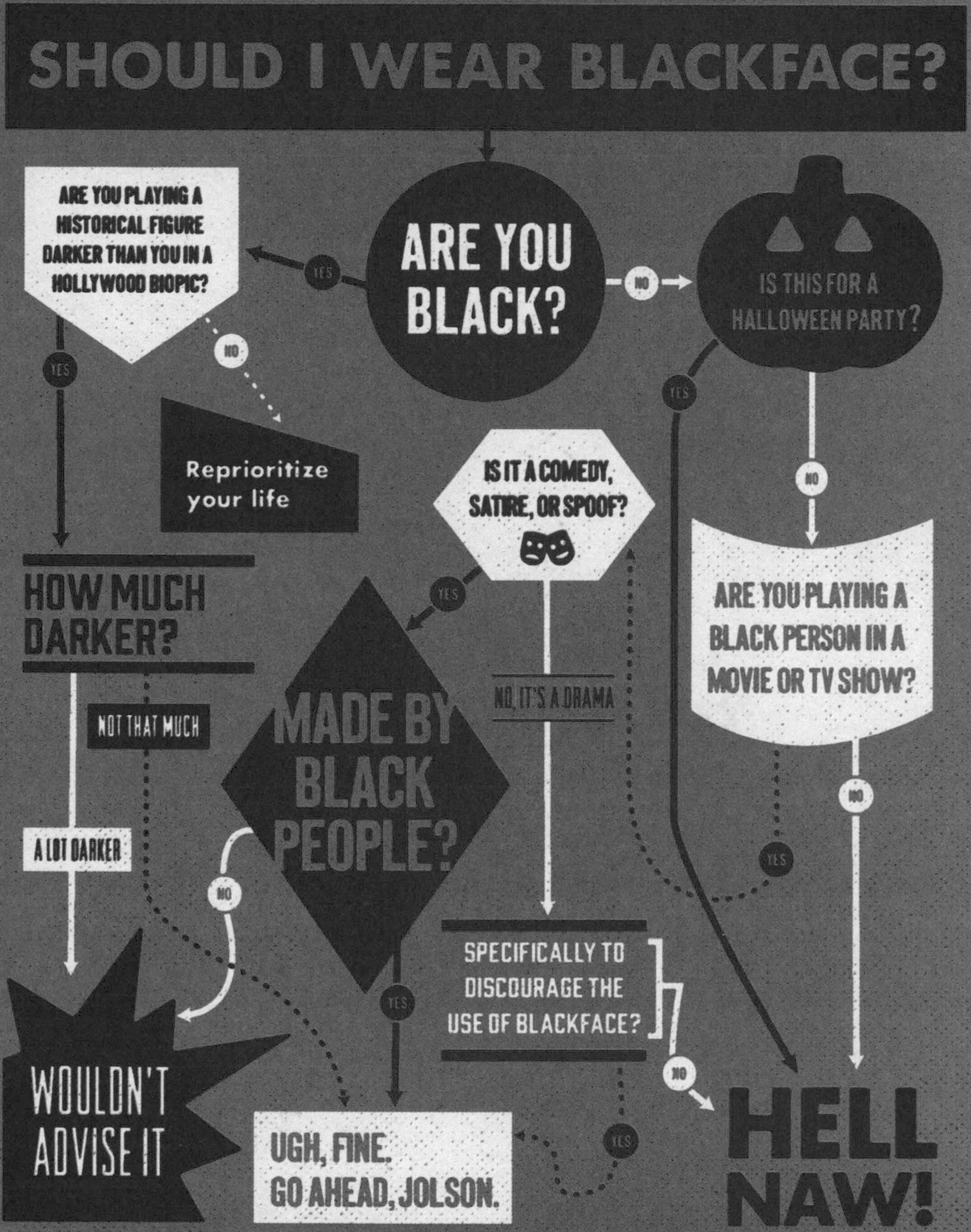

SHOULD I WEAR BLACKFACE?

ARE YOU BLACK?

ARE YOU PLAYING A HISTORICAL FIGURE DARKER THAN YOU IN A HOLLYWOOD BIOPIC? — YES

NO → Reprioritize your life

IS THIS FOR A HALLOWEEN PARTY? — NO

YES

IS IT A COMEDY, SATIRE, OR SPOOF?

HOW MUCH DARKER?

NOT THAT MUCH

A LOT DARKER

YES — **MADE BY BLACK PEOPLE?**

NO, IT'S A DRAMA

ARE YOU PLAYING A BLACK PERSON IN A MOVIE OR TV SHOW?

NO

NO

YES

SPECIFICALLY TO DISCOURAGE THE USE OF BLACKFACE?

YES

NO

WOULDN'T ADVISE IT

UGH, FINE. GO AHEAD, JOLSON.

HELL NAW!

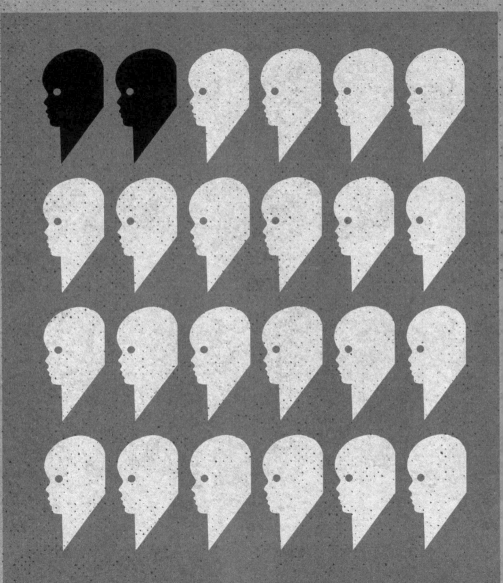

The Minimum Requirement of Black Friends Needed to Not Seem Racist Has Been Raised to Two

OR, ESCAPING THE TOKEN TRAP

OUR PEOPLE are terribly sorry for the inconvenience, but yes: One will no longer cut it. The era of the token black person has overstayed its welcome. Trying to convince prospective new students of color that they will not feel isolated at your campus? You will need to add another black person to the student life section of your college brochure. Want to capitalize on the millions of black women you just now discovered have TVs and a penchant for sophisticated drama thanks to the success of *Scandal*? You will now need more than one sassy black secretary to round out the cast of your office-based dramedy. Yes, this new rule extends to children's cartoons, ensemble superhero comics, groupings of Girl Scouts on boxes of cookies, and those WE'RE HIRING signs at Starbucks.

Though it used to be having a token black friend was a perfectly acceptable way to prove open-mindedness, white hipsters in Los Angeles and New York have raised the bar significantly. Thanks to vinyl shops, the resurgence of classic hip-hop, and the appropriation of skateboard culture by black teenagers, white early adapters on the coasts are collecting a staggering number of black friends, up to three in some cases! Which means the media needs to catch up. And while black folks were willing to tolerate the one-is-enough quotient up to this point, the jig is up. As was remarked by the loquacious

Buggin' Out in Spike Lee's seminal film *Do the Right Thing*, we will be needing some more brothers up on the wall. *Today.*

Beyond fleshing out the appearance of diversity in advertising and entertainment, it is recommended that white people also look to add some more black people to their lives. Not that we want to be hunted or acquired like rare stamps, but there's no denying that when one's circle of friends is expanded, so too is one's worldview.

Before you set out to add black friends to your circle, it's important to note who does *not* count. This may come as a surprise to you, but Oprah is not your friend.[9] Yes, she talks to you often and seems to have just the right solution to your deepest and most sacred childhood wounds, but you have not actually met her in person. Other television personalities including rappers, news anchors, and fictional characters, no matter how much you relate to them, do not count as your friend either. Prince is your spirit animal? Fantastic. Has he made you pancakes in his paisley house? If not, then you are not his friend.

Now, white readers may be saying, "How dare you minimize the relationship I have with my black friend!" Listen, hypothetical white person, your friendship with Jamal at work *does* count. The

---

[9] The author admits that there is a chance that Oprah may actually be a personal friend of yours. If that is the case, please tell her about me. I would really like to receive one of her favorite things. Also I'd like to have Iyanla Vanzant and La Toya Jackson (stars of the OWN television network) over for brunch. Oprah can come too. And you, I suppose . . .

times you spent playing basketball, arguing over whether to order the spicy or extra-spicy hot wings, and living vicariously through Jamal's anecdotes about sex with black women do count for something. The problem is, you've often confused Jamal with Steve, the other black guy at work. Take that in. There is a good chance you have confused your bbff[10] Jamal with another black guy at work. To be fair, both of these guys do have the same haircut, but Steve is a different person. He loathes hot wings. When it comes to sports, Steve couldn't tell you the difference between a Cav and a Cub, and Steve's insatiable penchant for white women is becoming a bone of contention for his sisters. If Jamal weren't your only black friend, you would've been able to spot the differences immediately.

50 Shades of Black

When you befriend multiple black people, it's a lot harder to confuse one for the other. This is because having more than one black friend automatically loosens the often subconscious grip of race-based assumptions that leads to stereotypes. You see, black people come in all different shades, beliefs, and hairstyles. Blackness encompasses everything from Michelle Obama to Missy Elliot. It's as wide as the chasm between Flavor Flav and Colin Powell. In-

---

[10] Best Black Friend Forever.

creasing your black friendship circle even to just two will immediately lay waste to that subconscious belief that all black people are either like (a) the ones on television or (b) the one existing friend/colleague already in your life. It will also stimulate and challenge your worldview with an influx of interesting and diverse points of view. In addition to the benefits mentioned above, there is another one associated with befriending us. Your one black friend is lonely. It is exhausting to be the only one in your life to explain things such as Affirmative Action and Black Twitter.[11]

Diversifying Your Blackfolio

Making friends with new black people can be easy and fun. You can find black people at your local grocer, at the post office, on an interstate train, even on Facebook. Relax when you encounter a black person. Try not to blurt, "Whattup my brotha?" or "Yasss, girlfriend, how you doin'?," as that's not how you normally talk.[12] Just be yourself and recognize that despite the difference in your appearances, the odds are just as likely that you will have as many

---

[11] The phenomenon that describes the increase of trending hashtags like #ByeFelicia and #SnatchedAtTheRoot that seems to occur when white people stop tweeting about Justin Bieber and go to sleep.

[12] If that is your natural God-given Caucasian speaking voice, TLC has a reality show contract for you! What are you doing reading this book?

things in common with this black person as with any person you're likely to meet. Being able to reference elements of black culture can be helpful, but don't force it. There's no need to quote *The Autobiography of Malcolm X* while in line to buy toilet paper. Save that for two whiskeys deep into your second or third hangout, when it doesn't feel so desperate. Remember everything you've learned about not touching black hair without permission (I've got a chapter on that) and that at the end of the day, black people are just like you, except subjugated to near constant racial microaggressions and prejudices!

TOKENS

It's sometimes hard to tell whether you and your friends are hanging out because your interests align, or simply because you make them feel more cultured. What's more confusing is that most people don't even realize they're being patronizing by inviting their black friend along because they're "so cool", or they're "sure to know people who have drugs."

So how do you know if your differences are being appropriately celebrated, or exotized by your "friends"? Conversely, how do you know when you are treating your friends like a house negro? Find out if you are a token, or if you've made a token out of a friend by taking the Token Quizzes!

Are You the Token Black Friend?

DO YOUR FRIENDS . . .	YES	NO
. . . get sullen when you muse about possibly getting rid of your natural hairstyle?		
. . . ask you to "go first" while investigating a strange noise during a camping trip?		
. . . laugh after everything you say? Like, *everything*?		
. . . yell "You go, girl!" at you often?		
. . . only invite you to go shopping, clubbing, or to diversity seminars?		
. . . show little interest in you after group selfies are taken?		
. . . have no interest in your hopes, dreams, and fears?		
. . . play underground hip-hop only when you get in the car?		
. . . feel the need to explain to you what Whole Foods is?		
. . . always yell out, "It's okay, he's with us!" when entering a 7-Eleven with you?		
. . . refer to you and only you as "bro" or "boo"?		
. . . only try to hook you up with people of your race?		
. . . always insist that you make the playlist?		

If you answered yes to six or more of these, you may be a token black friend. If you answered no to six or more, you may still be a token. Be ever vigilant.

Are You Tokening Your Black Friends?

DO YOU . . .	YES	NO
. . . find yourself earnestly bringing up Kwanzaa?		
. . . tag your black friend on every Barack Obama Instagram post?		
. . . wink at your black friends when there is watermelon at a party?		
. . . ask your black friends about life in the hood *before* being told where they grew up?		
. . . only text your black friend when you need more weed?		
. . . only say "yo" around your black friends?		
. . . decline an invitation to your black friend's birthday party because you assume you'll be the only white person there?		
. . . go out of your way to lie about the impact *Boyz N the Hood* has had on your life?		
. . . ask your black friends to give their opinions when the topic of inner-city racism is discussed with others?		
. . . go out of your way to tell other people that your black friend loves you?		
. . . go out of your way to pretend to celebrate Black History Month?		
. . . lie about preferring *The Wiz* to *The Wizard of Oz*?		

If you answered yes to six or more of these, you may be marginalizing your black friends. If you answered no to six or more, you may still be marginalizing them. Check to see if your fingers are in their hair.

WHO'S BLACK?

Like a Rorschach version of "Where's Waldo?" this test will help you snuff out any latent stereotype-based racism you might still hold! Sounds like fun, right? Simply pick out which figures in the pictures at right represent a black person. The key will let you know if you're racist, not racist, or cuspy.

Did you find the black people in the images, or are you totes racist? Check your selections against the key below.

1) This is a famous black pop star on tour (not racist) 2) A lovely rendering of a black man accepting an Oscar (not racist) 3) A white reality star with lip injections (cuspy) 4) A drug addict smoking from a really weird crack pipe (racist) 5) A well-to-do black business owner giving his wife a box of chocolates (not racist) 6) Possibly the scarecrow character from The Wiz (cuspy) 7) Korean Michael Jackson impersonator (cuspy) 8) Gorilla in a pantsuit (racist) 9) A black politician giving a speech on childhood obesity (not racist) 10) An extra in a scene from The Help (cuspy) 11) A frightening theme park character (cuspy) 12) A white pop star rehearsing (cuspy) 13) An Asian basketball player (racist) 14) How dare you! (racist)

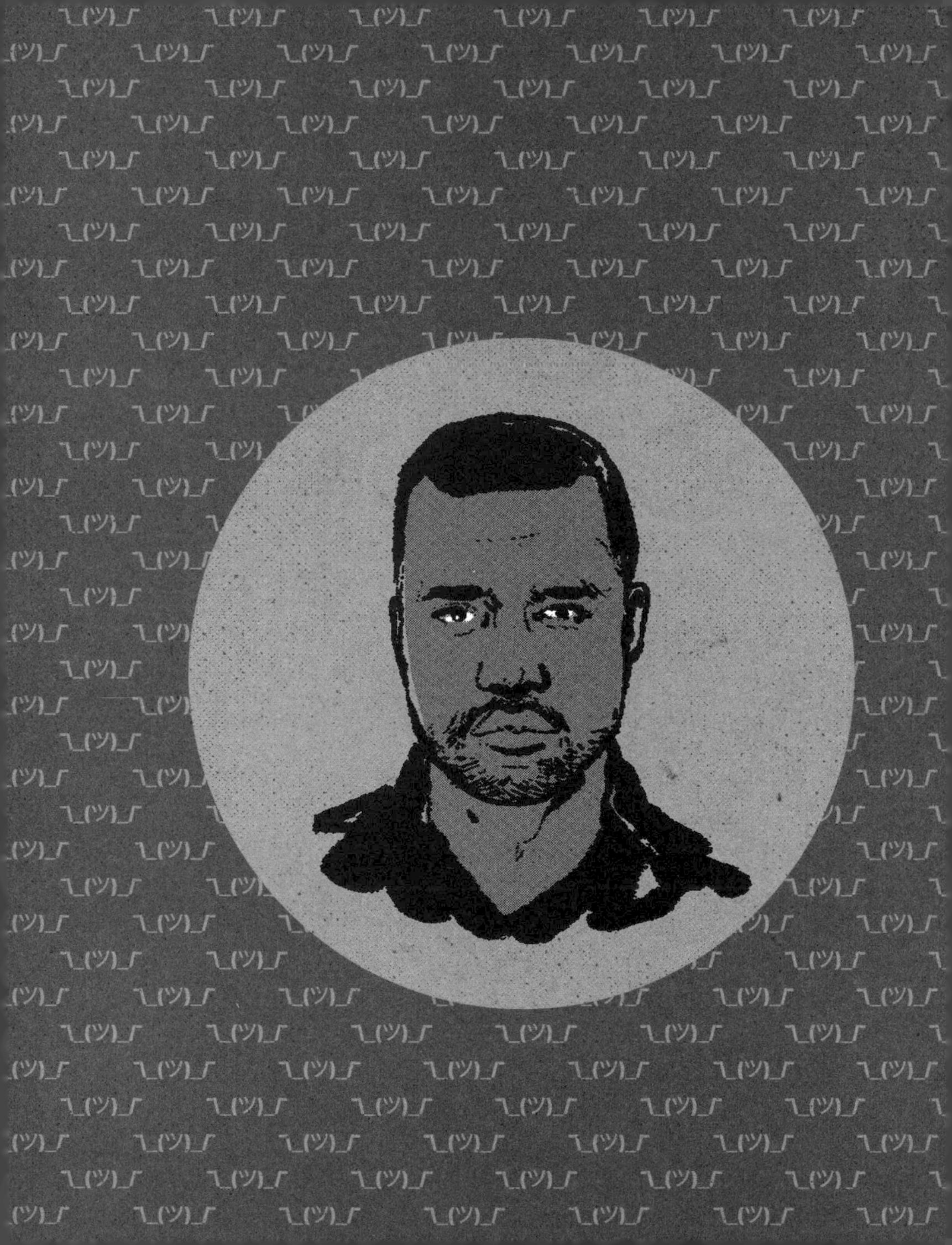

We Don't Know Why Kanye West Did That

OR, SPEAKING ON BEHALF OF THE BLACK RACE

?

DIVINING BLACK CULTURE

XIX

THE BLACKSPERT

THE **BEHAVIOR** of Kanye West is endlessly fascinating for most people. On the one hand, he's a groundbreaking and relentless innovator in the worlds of music and fashion. On the other hand, he's a modern-day philosopher expounding truisms on Twitter, such as "I could never do stand-up 'cause I tell jokes better when I'm sitting" or "Sometimes I fuk with my Timbs on." One day Kanye's words will be organized into sutras and debated over by monks, in time becoming the basis for the world's primary religion. But until then, no one will truly understand exactly what a rarefied pop genius such as Kanye West is doing or talking about. Ever. Not even black people.

Black folks are often individually regarded as the authority on every facet of black culture and the people who create it, but it's exhausting for most black people to constantly be relied upon as the go-to official spokesnegro. Sure, a ton of black people who voted in 2012 voted for Obama, but so did most white people who voted. We are not suddenly experts on the Israeli/Palestinian crisis or the ethics of drone warfare just because the president is black. Some of us just want to spend the news hour nursing addictions to alcohol and Xbox like the rest of the country.

You may find a debate partner with a startlingly profound amount of "research-based" opinions about the details of Tupac's murder and the deeper meaning behind "Electric Relaxation" by A Tribe Called Quest, but their knowledge isn't solely a consequence of their being black. That's just where their interests lie. To turn to the nearest representative of the race to ask a question or passionately discuss an issue without considering whether or not that person is interested or qualified is to set you both up for failure.

Of course, black folks have a role to play in this as well. It's often to our advantage to be able to interject the supposed black opinion in meetings or at dinner parties. Explaining in a marketing meeting, for instance, that watching BET is not the only thing black people do in their free time has helped get dozens of black people promotions, albeit without pay increases. Millions of white folks have been charmed across dinner tables by the urban-tinged anecdotes of their black friends. Whether they are relaying sacred celebrity knowledge and insight from black blogs such as bossip.com and theybf.com or explaining the etymology of new slang terms such as "ratchet," The Black Friend™ too gets a little something out of being thought of as a "black authority." But this is a thought trap for both groups.

Speaking personally, many of my Jewish friends know far more about popular black culture than I do.[13] Their knowledge tends

---

[13] Evidenced by the glossary of terms in this book.

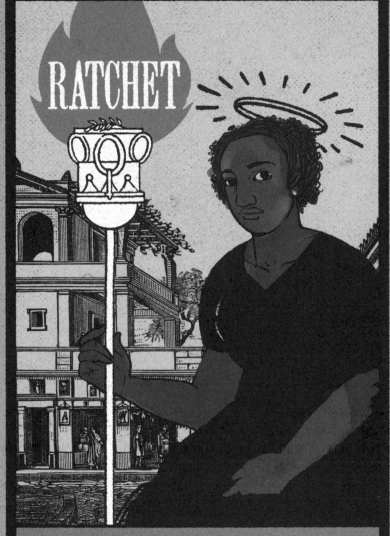

DIVINING BLACK CULTURE

RATCHET

THE ORACLE OF SLANG

to gloss over important civil-rights-related news and focuses, instead, on obscure rap lyrics and vintage Richard Pryor jokes, but still. There are certain situations where they would fare much better at playing (or at least scripting) the role of The Black Friend™ than I would. Unfortunately, relaying everyday mundane observations from my actual so-called black experience just doesn't have the same punch to it over dinner as reenacting the blind KKK leader scene from *Chapelle's Show*.

It's important to keep in mind the following: The pressure to be quintessentially black in every moment, whether it comes from the outside world or is self-imposed, keeps black people from being our authentic selves.

In reference to the hypothetical marketing meeting I alluded to earlier, your black coworker could blow your mind and positively influence where ad dollars are spent in a business meeting by stating what should be the obvious: Black people don't all watch the same one channel. However, this black coworker's real expertise may be in viral social marketing—a talent being wasted in favor of being the black spokesperson. Your Black Friend™ at the party might just be dying to discuss with you the documentary on Nirvana he saw on Netflix instead of yet again explaining the differences between Idris Elba and Chiwetel Ejiofor. But the way things are going, neither of you may have the pleasure.

Of course, everyone's interests and personalities are affected by their cultural and racial influences. This book relies upon a number of racially specific touch points and archetypes, such as the idea that black people come in one of four versions[14] or that we are all fans of Michael Jackson.[15] But the truth is, like humanity everywhere, black people just want to be recognized in all our complexity. Ultimately, life is most fun when our identities are allowed to *evolve* in the quest to figure out who we are, a liberty not always encouraged for people of color.

So the next time you see a black person, ask them a non-black-specific question. You might be surprised at the response!

---

[14] See "Paperbag Tests."

[15] This one is true. Probably. See "Here's the Thing about Michael Jackson."

R
U A
POST-
RACIST

—————

A QUIZ

—————

Are You a Post-Racist?

The idea that we have somehow evolved beyond racism is downright contagious in American culture. Sure, it's easy to be blinded by strides in civil rights, the "Carlton Dance," and reruns of *The Cosby Show*, but racism is still very much a problem. For one thing, most of the civil rights black people have gained such as voting, freedom of speech, and the right *not* to be shot for no reason, don't seem to apply in some parts of the country. Like Florida!

While it's nice to hope that years of oppression could be wiped away by Oprah Winfrey's getting a network and white people reluctantly going to see *12 Years a Slave,* unfortunately it isn't so. In truth the idea of "post-racism" is really just a denial of racism. But how do you know if you are suffering from this common, and sometimes fatal, delusion? Could it be that while you are not a racist, you might be a . . . post-racist?

Take this helpful quiz to find out!

1. Dr. Dre just became a billionaire, one of the very few billionaires of African descent in America, in fact! What's your reaction?

   a. Shock that this *just now* happened. *The Chronic* album cover has been hanging on your wall since the mid-nineties. How was he not a billionaire already?

b. Satisfaction that all of those whiny liberals who claim the black man can't get ahead will finally be silenced.

c. Indifference. Of course he became a billionaire. Just like P. Diddy and Bill Cosby, he's talented and beloved.

d. Agitated because this further proves the disparity of wealth between the races. Of the 1,645 living billionaires, only nine are black and only two are American. *That* should be the headline.

2. In 2013, Lupita Nyong'o, a then relatively unknown actress of Kenyan descent, won an Academy Award for her role as Patsey in the film *12 Years a Slave*. How'd you react when you heard the news?

a. I stood and applauded in the middle of my Oscar-viewing party. Hollywood and the standards of beauty in American culture will be forever changed by this monumental win!

b. I never saw the film; it's too intense. But June Squibb was robbed!

c. It was great to see a talented and stunning actress gain notoriety for good work, even if it was for playing a slave.

d. I had to have a drink to calm my rage over Hollywood's obsession with brutalized black women in order to celebrate the very deserved victory for Lupita. I continue to look forward to the next time an American black actor is awarded for playing a complex and interesting role unrelated to slavery, domestic work, inner-city violence, and/or contracting AIDS.

3. Why do black kids in predominantly white middle schools tend to sit together in the cafeteria?

a. At that age, where else will they be able to practice rap battling?

b. Because as much as black people like to point the finger at society, they are as responsible for segregation as anybody else.

c. They probably share common cultural interests.

d. Identifying with a particular group is a necessary survival tactic when confronted with a majority culture's often misguided perception of your race and ethnicity. Finding others who share that burden can be a comforting respite, particularly during these developmental years.

4. During a constructive conversation about racism in America, what role does "class discrimination" play?

   a. It moves the conversation from "black vs. white" to the more important issue in this country of "rich vs. poor."

   b. It dismantles a ludicrous cry of racism from black people, who are doing fine, by pointing out that the poor in this country have it worse regardless of race!

   c. It adds a vital layer to a very important discussion.

   d. It totally changes the subject and reduces the experience of people of color in this country to one that can be shared by white people too and thereby deflects any guilt or blame.

5. What is the purpose of celebrating Black History Month?

   a. Taking time to remember the bomb-ass contributions black people have had on society, such as the ice cream scoop and yo mama jokes.

   b. Liberals can feel good about themselves by calling out the contributions of one group of people who continue to insist they don't get special treatment.

   c. It allows McDonald's to resurrect the McRib and get away with vaguely racist targeted advertising.

   d. It provides, in equal parts, a way to uplift young black children to aspire to greatness and a way for white people to absolve themselves of guilt by mentioning George Washington Carver while making a peanut butter and jelly sandwich.

See Where You Fall on the Post-Racist Spectrum

Match the majority of your answers to each category.

a = Post-Racist

b = Institutional Post-Racist

c = Post Post-Racist

d = Freedom Fighter

A) Post-Racist: Your enjoyment and involvement in aspects of black culture are appreciated but may have obscured your awareness of racism. You are severely at risk of wearing blackface at a Halloween party or not understanding why this book exists. Consider watching even more MSNBC.

B) Institutional Post-Racist: Your contribution to the propagation of racism is matched only by your enthusiastic insistence that it doesn't exist. Consider a job at Fox News, running as a Tea Party candidate for senate, or leaving the country and never coming back.

C) Post Post-Racist: While you are slightly oblivious to the ways in which people of color are still challenged by racism, you can see there are areas where society can be improved. Consider increasing the number of black friends in your life.

D) Freedom Fighter: The good news is you are adequately aware of how racism still operates in America, either from experience or sound education. Congratulations! The bad news is you are well on your way to clinical depression and/or joining an extremist group. Consider adding long walks to your day and reading the "I Have a Dream" speech before bedtime.

It's not that I'm blind.

Sometimes I'm just not paying attention.

Here's the Thing about Michael Jackson

about

Michael Jackson

OR, TREASON IN
THE KINGDOM OF POP

In 2014 the results of a groundbreaking study conducted by Harvard University over a period of two decades were finally revealed. Titled "What Do Black People Talk About?," it verified what most black people anecdotally know: Black people are almost always discussing Michael Jackson (93 to 94 percent of the time, according to the study).[16]

The reasons for this should be obvious. Michael Jackson was the most talented human being to ever moonwalk across the face of the planet. That he happened to be black is a source of tremendous pride for our people. He also possessed magical powers. (No one else but black women can lay claim to this unique talent; see the chapter on hair.) The sidewalk would light up when he walked on it. He could time-travel to Black Egypt at will, gang violence would evaporate into choreographed dance battles in his presence, and somehow he could turn into robots, cars, and Tyra Banks whenever he so desired. These, as far as my people and I are concerned, are verifiable facts.

Most white people are on the same page with this one, but occasionally a white person has the need to interject an off-color[17] comment into a conversation about Michael Jackson, either ex-

---

[16] This is not a real study, but I really wanted to back my opinion up with a fact, so I made one up, or what some Fox News correspondents refer to as "reporting the news."

[17] Freudian slip.

aggerating his various cosmetic alterations or his alleged crimes. After years of research into this, I've come to understand that this urge is based either on subconscious guilt over Elvis's appropriation of black music or unprocessed rage over O. J. Simpson.

If your immediate thought when I noted above that Michael Jackson "happened to be black," was something like *Yeah, until 1987,* then you may be feeling the effects of aforementioned guilt/rage. As his R. Kelly–penned 1995 hit song exclaimed, you are not alone, and hopefully what follows can correct your thinking on the issue.

As was evidenced by the disparate mix of skin colors seen in the Huxtable children on *The Cosby Show,* black people come in many different shades. Michael Jackson taught us that a *single* black person can also come in many different shades. Nothing weird about that! If musical artists from Madonna to Katy Perry are to be praised for reinventing themselves every album or so by trading in cone bras for candy bras, Michael Jackson must be praised for giving you every gradation of black melanoma from a Miles Davis skintone to one that approaches that of the guys from Milli Vanilli, sometimes in the same decade. Sometimes, as is the case with "Black or White," in the same video. Yes, black people's interest in and praise of Michael Jackson may appear both irrational and insatiable, but actually it is not. It's the normal response.

The best way for white people to discuss Michael with new black friends is to praise him, but not with a predictable throwaway comment about *Off the Wall* being the best of his albums. A great way to praise the King of Pop, even if you've yet to connect with your latent feelings of enthusiasm toward him, is to simply put your hand to your heart and act as if the swell of emotion within you is too profound to finish even a sentence. You will then be able to get away with comments such as "Man, he was just . . ." and "When I listen to his music I just . . ." while you work independently on removing your personal obstacles to loving him in a more specific way.

If you are in touch with your natural and God-given love for MJ already, it's time for you to move on to more advanced topics.

White people who can, for instance, passionately discuss the

influence that the album cuts on *Dangerous*—I'm thinking here of "She's Driving Me Wild"—had on the development of the musical genre new jack swing will instantly win the hearts of many a black person. The ability to coolly note the similarities between Jackson's hairstyle in the "Remember the Time" video and his sister Janet's in "Escapade" will do wonders for a white person enjoying R&B night at their favorite club. The brave white man at a party with the confidence to pontificate on the role Quincy Jones's jazz background played in the hook to "Liberian Girl" from *Bad* is liable to spontaneously get a black woman pregnant by night's end. Thus is the power of the Pop King.

Point is, being able to discuss your love for Michael Jackson in great detail is sure to get most black people to like and possibly even trust you. There are, of course, some exceptions here. Occasionally, you may encounter a black person who insists that they don't like Michael Jackson outside of the Motown era, or that they're more of a Prince fan. Be wary. These people are probably trying to trick you.

Stand sure in your love of Michael Jackson, whether you feel it or not. Even when a posthumous allegation is being levied against him in the media, you must force yourself to see that for what it is: institutionalized racism.

Still feeling doubtful? Listen to "Will You Be There" again. If that doesn't help, I'm all out of ideas. The chord progressions in that one song alone are the work of a genius. Don't even get me started on the glitter socks.

BLACK MYTH BUSTERS

Dancing

The time has come to come clean about this, white people. While I must admit there are a good number of you destroying the rhythmic intent of songs like "Single Ladies" and "Crank That (Soulja Boy)" across wedding dance floors all over America, the correlation between race and dance abilities is purely a myth. Thanks to the "positive stereotype" that all black people can dance, the reason you rarely see a black person dancing poorly is because they know better. They'd rather just sway subtly, nod their heads, and keep the mystique alive. White people don't have the same illusion to maintain and therefore feel freer to sway off beat and do that raise-the-roof hand thing.

A notable exception would be president Barack Obama, who unabashedly danced like a white lady with a white lady, Ellen, on her show in 2007, to "Crazy in Love." And to be honest, there's something kind of baller about a black man having the balls to do the white boy shuffle on national television.

No, it appears that rhythm is a learned trait. People coming up in a family in which dancing is common will naturally begin to pick it up, whether we're talking about voguing, Harlem shuffling, or Riverdancing. People with notoriously poor rhythm can improve, and people with good enough baseline skills can master almost any form of dance. Just like Justin Timberlake or crazy Natalie Portman in *Black Swan*.

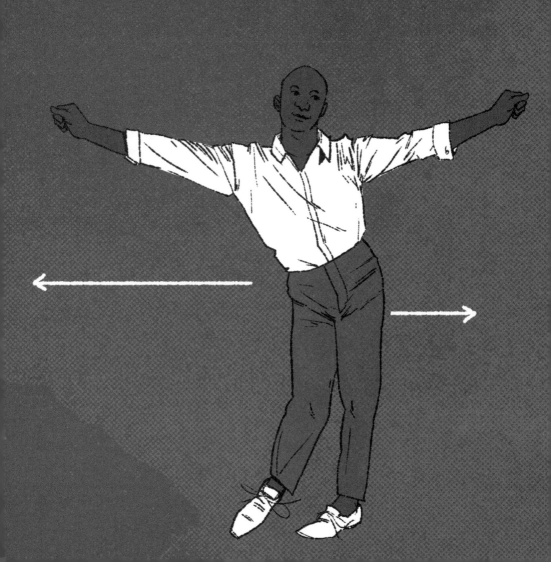

Why Does the White Version Do Better?

THE WIZ VS. THE WIZARD OF OZ

IN **2013,** the twerking trend reached critical mass in American pop culture when ~~record label publicity~~ outrage over Miley Cyrus dancing onstage with Robin Thicke at the 2013 *MTV Video Music Awards* show made headlines all over the blogosphere. During an *Ellen Show* appearance featuring Nicki Minaj, Ellen mused that Nicki had been "twerking for a long long time" and told her that the media wasn't "outraged when you did it." Nicki Minaj best summed up a centuries-old phenomenon of cultural appropriation when she responded, "You know, it's the white girl thing . . . If a white girl does something that seems to be, like, black . . . white people think, oh she must be cool, she doin' something black! But if a black person do a black thing, it ain't that poppin'." Well put, Nicki!

Despite being around for more than thirty years, and having made its pop music debut in 2000 with the seminal "Whistle While You Twurk" by the Ying Yang Twins, it wasn't until the move and term were popularized by Cyrus that the word "twerk" made the Oxford Dictionary Online. It seems as if there really is something about the white version of a black thing that's been around for a while that resonates more strongly with mass audiences, i.e., white people. Like the white iPhone, the white version of a thing is almost assured success.

This chapter isn't really meant to denigrate Miley Cyrus. If doing an alright twerk and making music with Pharrell furthers her professional aspirations, I'm all for it. As far as I know, black folks are not yet able to jointly apply for patents on things like twerking or jazz or spontaneously busting out into the chorus of "Weak" by SWV. So while it might be irritating to admit sometimes, everything we come up with culturally is up for grabs! We live in a postmodern era where reference to something that exists already is just another form of self-expression. Without the influences of postmodernism, we wouldn't have cultural gems such as Andy Warhol's *Campbell's Soup Cans* and Lady Gaga's meat dress.

It's difficult, for instance, to attack Madonna for taking voguing from the poverty-stricken black gay ball culture only to turn around and celebrate Digable Planets for constructing transcendent hip-hop out of odds and ends from vintage jazz records. But what is troubling is the unwillingness of mass popular culture to accept an idea unless it passes through a white filter. Like Elvis!

The Elvis Effect

Yes, I'm going to talk about Elvis. And I know that white folks are tired of hearing black people talk about Elvis, about how the King of Rock and Roll basically built his kingdom with a sound that was essentially created and refined in the black community. But what happened in the 1950s with rock and roll music, at times referred to as "race music" by persnickety white folks of the day, is emblematic. At a time when suburban white kids began to duck out of their sock hops and ice cream socials and other generic white-people-in-the-fifties activities to secretly listen to Chuck Berry records, singers like Elvis and Bill Haley provided an invaluable service. Like Kidz Bop does for aggressively homeschooled children, I'm guessing, Elvis allowed white kids to enjoy elements of "socially unacceptable" music in a more acceptable package. White people discovered rock and roll via Elvis and marveled at what to them was a "new sound." Elvis, an incredibly shrewd and talented artist, became the King. Little Richard's penchant for wigs and eyeliner be damned.

The tradition in music continues to this day. The success of New Edition was eventually eclipsed by its white clone, New Kids on the Block. Eminem has sold more records than any other rap artist in history and Justin Timberlake's fusion of Michael Jackson and Bobby Brown is repeatedly met with bigger fanfare than Usher's. Now, there are some notable exceptions. The success of moguls such as Berry Gordy and Clive Davis relied on their ability to take black music sung by actual black people and present it in a way that older white people in the middle of the country could handle. Yes, technically the Supremes were singing rhythm and blues, but thanks to European wigs and Diana Ross's deceptively casual singing voice, white people everywhere were humming "Baby Love" without short-circuiting.

Columbusing

The phenomenon that describes the runaway success that occurs for things culturally appropriated by white people was brilliantly

summed up by CollegeHumor in their 2014 viral video "Colum-busing." In it, an enthusiastic white hipster insists to his black friend that he discovered a hip bar in Bed-Stuy. When his black friend tells him that many people knew about the bar before he did, his white friend retorts by saying that he "Colum-bused it"; i.e., discovered it for white people before a gaggle of hip white people flooded in. Since it seems that being Colum-bused is a prerequisite for the success of some things, here is a hastily compiled and incomplete list of things/people whose popularity was blown out of obscurity once white people discovered and appropriated it:

- Quinoa
- Harlem Shake
- Saying "YOLO"
- Yoga
- Wearing colorful Navajo prints from the 1990s
- Singing R&B music after 2011
- Authentic Mexican Cuisine
- Hummus
- Eastern Medicine
- Zumba
- Food Trucks
- Nick Cannon

Could it be that the white masses in this country are really that unwilling to try new foods, fitness routines, and musical trends without a white person "discovering" and interpreting it first? It would seem so.

The Black Version

Shockingly, cultural appropriation in the reverse direction is met with mixed to discouraging results. It seems that often the black version of an existing white thing is almost always a letdown. "Colored Only" bathrooms, for instance. The term "separate but not equal" articulated the observation that whether it was education, bus seats, or water fountains, the version meant for black people always seemed subpar, at least in popularity if not creativity.

Walt Disney's animated epic *Snow White and the Seven Dwarfs* was greeted with critical acclaim, recognition at the Academy Awards, and the financial success that helped secure Disney's cinematic empire. The black version created in 1943 by Merry Melodies called *Coal Black and de Sebben Dwarfs* is seven minutes of animated stereotypes featuring a character called Prince Chawmin' who answers the heroine Coal Black's lament "Some folks think I's kinda dumb, but I know someday ma prince will come" with a rollicking "I has come!" Also (thankfully) forgotten by history is the 1944 animated black version of a popular classic called *Goldilocks and the Jivin' Bears* featuring cheeky narration such as "These black bears, they neva went to school, but when it come to jivin' they ain't nobody's fool."

Now, creatively, things are a bit better when actual black people are involved in the creation of the "black version." Nevertheless, most people prefer to go over the rainbow with Judy Garland instead of Diana Ross, my uncomplicated adoration of *The Wiz* notwithstanding.

To be fair, icons such as Prince, Spike Lee, Tiger Woods, and Darius Rucker have all successfully reclaimed spheres of culture that were at the time reserved only for white artists (glam rock, art-house movies, golf, and country music, respectively), but this is usually the exception and not the rule.

What I'm basically trying to say is, can we have skateboarding? Céline Dion? Organic farming? Something? I mean, we gave you classic hip-hop!

BLACK MYTH BUSTERS

Sports

This one is complicated. It is true that ethnicity is a factor in the genetically programmed abilities of an individual, and it can't be denied that 80 percent of the NBA and more than 60 percent of the NFL is made up of black players. Black people also hold every major running record in the world. This is largely due to the fact that white people have been in pursuit of us for centuries—either for slave labor or chasing us away from their white daughters. That was a joke, but one supported by anthropologist William Montague Cobb. In 1936 he argued that black people had greater physical capacities because their ancestors were able to survive physical hardships long enough to procreate, thus passing along the genes that gave them an upper hand.

It is true that people of West African descent tend to have more fast-twitch fibers. It's also true that outside of basketball, football, track, and boxing, white people globally dominate athletics. (See, for example, sports such as soccer and snow polo, which the Internet assures me is a thing.)

Overall, just like white people, most black people are shockingly unathletic. If one of us happens to have the desire to run for a living combined with the right "African twitch fibers," watch out, white competitors! However, the odds are much more likely that our "running" is confined to a twenty-minute treadmill sesh twice a week at the gym, promptly followed by an order of the pad Thai we "earned" like the rest of America.

Contrary to popular belief,
the combination of a black man and skill at basketball
is far from a universal constant.

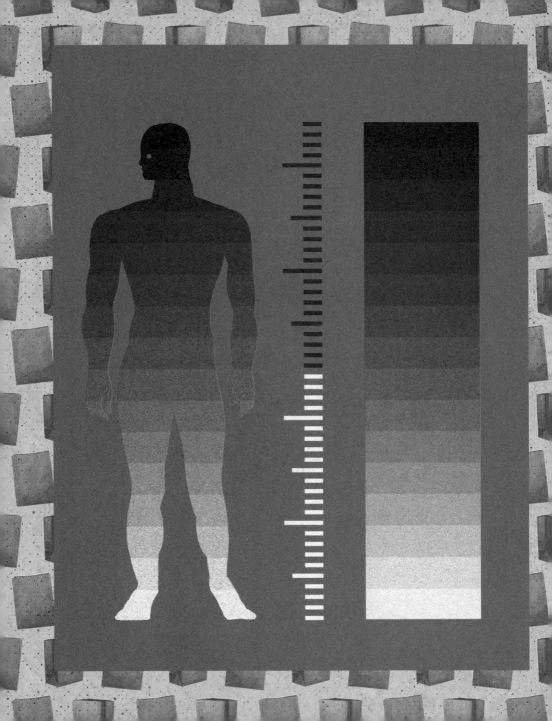

There Are Shades of Black

OR, HOW BLACK ARE YOU?

AT A CERTAIN POINT, many black people have an experience that makes us question our own blackness. Whether opting out of being the fifth in an impromptu pickup game of basketball because we never learned to dribble or admitting to a friend he/she never watched *The Wire,* there is an acute pain associated with failing to live up to the publicly revered cultural assumptions about black folk.

There are almost as many opinions of what constitutes being "authentically black" *within* the black community as there are black people. What makes one more "black," knowing who Bayard Rustin is, or having a collection of Air Jordan Retros? Owning *Roots* or *Django Unchained*? Working on the Obama campaign or knowing Kendrick Lamar was going to be a thing before anybody else did? What if all the above describes you, but you also have a fondness for the television show *Friends*? What if none of the above describes you, but you possess an actual Mahalia Jackson record on vinyl? How black are you? And does narrowly defining yourself so that you meet the cultural assumptions of others bring meaning to your life?

Well, of course it does! And fortunately, discovering how black you are is as easy as taking the Paper Bag Test at the end of this section. The test is named after the practice brown-skinned people used in the past to exclude other slightly more brown-skinned people from certain churches, dances, and employment opportunities. It was administered by holding a paper bag up to the face of anyone seeking admittance to said gathering to see which was darker. Colorism and segregation for dummies!

My version of the test, based in part on a similar test administered in the film *Dear White People*, is also designed to rate your blackness even if you're not actually black. Yes, despite the majority of this book advocating the idea that a person's identity is multifaceted and done a disservice by being boiled down into lazy, convenient stereotypes, you can trust this test to accurately tell you absolutely everything there is to know about yourself, without even a hint of irony or sarcasm!

THE PAPER BAG TEST

INSTRUCTIONS

STEP ONE

Taking the Paper Bag Test is easy. Simply read each hypothetical situation and see which responses resonate (or don't) with how you would typically respond:

1. For the response you would most likely give, mark a "7."
2. For the next closest, mark a "5."
3. For the third closest, mark a "3."
4. For the response you would least likely give, mark a "1."

STEP TWO

Transfer your numerical responses to this grid and total up the numbers for columns A, B, C, and D. You may want to re-create the grid on a separate sheet of paper so as not to ruin your copy of this book.

	A	B	C	D
1				
2				
3				
4				
TOTALS				

STEP THREE

Tally up the totals at the bottom of the grid. The letter that corresponds with the high number is your primary state of blackness, which will be expounded upon after you make your way through the test!

The Tip Test

You and a friend finally get a table at one of the most exclusive restaurants in town. Being the only colored folks in the establishment, you are keenly aware that your white waiter has gone around to every other table but yours taking orders, checking in, and making polite conversation. When he finally comes over, he's very quick to interrupt your order of sparkling water to warn you that it "costs extra." He also interjects when you order the pork loin that "the establishment doesn't carry hot sauce." You'd have preferred it sans the side of racism but the pork is fine, even though you could've binge-watched an entire season of *Orange Is the New Black* in the time it took you to get it. So what goes through your head when it's time to leave the tip?

A Motherfuck that waiter AND John Wayne. I'm leaving the dustiest dimes I can find in my pocket for that shitty-ass service.

B I resent the stereotype held by this misguided waiter who obviously ignored us because he believes that African Americans don't tip. I will leave 20 percent; no, 25 percent just to prove that I can.

C I'll leave precisely 15 percent, which is standard but lets the friend I'm with know I'm indignant about the way we were treated.

D What do I do again? Double the tax? Move the decimal? Isn't there an app for this?

The Twerk Test

You walk into your friend Becca's house party to exclamations of "HAAAAAAY!" and "NOW THE PARTY CAN START!," all from well-meaning white friends who are hoping you will be the one to get an impromptu dance floor in the living room started. Obviously, you need a drink first. As you sip on Grey Goose and flat Sprite from a red plastic cup, there are cries for you to join the dance floor as Marvin Gaye's "Got to Give It Up" comes on. Difficult though it is, you resist. That is, until you hear it . . . the black song du jour. Every year there's a new one. It's the smash urban hit with the repetitive beat and a choreographed, viral dance the entire free world and, possibly, a men's correctional facility or two, seem compelled to replicate via YouTube. All of the partygoers are practically pulling you onto the dance floor, expecting you will teach them how to do it. You know the moves. Truth be told, you look amazing doing them. How do you respond?

A   Insist that you ain't nobody's Sambo and refuse to tap-dance for these people, while you grab a bottle of rum and head for the door.

B   Resist the seductive call of the beat and insist that you've never heard of this song, as you're going through a bit of a Mumford & Sons phase at the moment.

C   Twerk, Dougie, and Superman Dat Ho until you are blue in the face. You're a motherfucking god to these people.

D   Depending on how stimulating a conversation you struck up over your Sprite, vodka, and potato chips, you weigh whether you feel like dancing at this moment.

Twerk

The Birthday Test

It's been an amazing year for you and you decide to throw yourself a hot birthday party at a hip local bar. You've booked a DJ to spin your favorite jams from today and back in the day and secured the dance floor for the night. There's even a cocktail named after you, thanks to a liquor sponsor. You're looking your best, and you're all set to have the time of your life. Where are your white friends?

A What white friends? Does the bouncer count? 'Cause I think he's Puerto Rican at best.

B My white friends? You mean *my friends*? They're all around me as we sway to the latest electropop stylings from bands like Röyksopp and Metronomy while deciding when to break out the Cards Against Humanity set.

C Had a really nice dinner with Carol, Travis, and Brad before the party. They probably won't enjoy this hood shit that's about to go down anyway. Not sure if I remembered to send Kurt the invite, but we'll probably go for drinks after work next week.

D Why would I make a distinction between my white and black friends? Everybody's here having a good time, though I must admit a bit of a shift occurred around me on the dance floor when the DJ switched from "Poison" by Bell Biv DeVoe to "Girls Just Wanna Have Fun."

The Obama Test

You find yourself in yet another conversation about Barack Obama with a generally liberal white person. Despite agreeing that he has made significant progress in a number of areas, you find yourself in the familiar position of being expected to defend President Obama against the claim that he didn't "do enough" with regard to healthcare and immigration reform. To be honest, you're not terribly familiar with the political intricacies of the issue at hand but somehow you've found yourself in this rather impassioned conversation. Finally, your white friend says, "Plain and simple, he campaigned on the promise of overhauling healthcare and immigration reform, and ending illegal global warfare, but he didn't. How do you account for this?"

Well? How do you?

A   Racism, muthafucka!

B   You agree that while candidate Obama inspired you with hopes of a newer and better America, it appears he just didn't have it in him to accomplish his goals. Maybe we needed Hillary after all?

C   You shrug and offer a truce in the form of an "I don't know, man" before switching the subject to the game on television. You'll never lose love for Obama, but what's the point in arguing?

D   Admit that like any president, Obama accomplished only some of his campaign promises, and try to close on a statement of fact that you both can agree upon.

HOPE

I don't know, man.

Interpreting Your Results

You've taken the tests, now tally up your score! Because cat videos and the Kardashian iPad app have destroyed the short-term memory of everyone forty-five and under, here's a reminder of how to score the responses:

1. A "7" for the response you would most likely give
2. A "5" for for the next closest
3. A "3" for the third closest
4. A "1" for the response you would least likely give

Here's an example of a chart with the numbers tallied up. The letter column with the highest total at the bottom represents your primary trait. All of the traits are likely in you somewhere, but there are usually one or two states of blackness that dominate your personality, because all people should fit neatly into *Cosmo* Quiz–style personality tests.

	A	B	C	D
1	3	1	7	5
2	1	5	7	3
3	1	3	5	7
4	5	3	7	1
TOTALS	10	12	26	16

As you can see, "C" or "OOFTA" (see page 119) is this test-taker's primary state of blackness. What did you get and what does it mean? Tally up, consult the next pages, and say hello to your blackness.

The Traits

A = ONE HUN-NED

If your primary trait was A, you are One Hun-ned, which basically means you are black as hell, just because. You revel in a righteous, militant state of black nationalism that you have no bones about wearing on your sleeve. Literally. Whether you are rocking a STRAIGHT OUTTA COMPTON T-shirt, or an actual dashiki, powerful elements of black identity are your default modes of self-expression. And this is a good thing. Far too many people of color have been made to be ashamed of their race, and you are doing your part to counteract that. While it is tempting to think of this state of blackness as the most authentic, a word of caution. You also may have some less-than-traditionally "black" characteristics that you are hiding from your friends, such as a preference for microgreens instead of collards and a secret stash of Willie Nelson records. Eventually, the mental pressure of filtering out aspects of your personality you deem to be not black enough will get the better of you, so it's best to integrate them now. No one worth your time will lose respect for you just because your favorite song from childhood is "Spice Up Your Life" and you have a thing for Jennifer Aniston movies. Support your community, but never at the expense of yourself!

B = NOSE JOB

If your primary trait was B, you might be a Nose Job, which means you actively underplay aspects of your black identity, either from fear of being pigeonholed or because they embarrass you. While you may or may not have actually had a nose job, your aesthetic choices from your fashion style to the music you listen to carry with them a conscious effort to disprove the cultural assumptions others may have about you based on your race. While some people might refer to you as "technically black" or "whitewashed," you are actually engaged in your own special kind of identity rebellion. However, if you tend to freeze up when you see the one other black person in the room while you're discussing *The Bachelor* or golf with your white friends, there may be an element of shame at play. If you're afraid the other black people you encounter will reject you for not being black enough, there's a chance you've rejected some aspect of yourself. Breathe and tell yourself it's okay that you secretly enjoy the taste of Kool-Aid and get the same guilty pleasure from *Girlfriends* reruns on BET that any sane human being would. Truly being free from the limits of a stereotype means you can enjoy aspects of it without fear it will engulf you!

C = OOFTA

If your primary trait was C, you are an OOFTA, or a black person who modulates their blackness up or down depending on the situation. The term was coined in the 1930s to describe jazz performers who played the then predominantly black music in a way that was palatable to white audiences. You have different speaking voices when you answer the phone, depending on the race of the person calling. You cultivate several sets of interests but share only some of them with the friend circle you happen to be in at the time. Your black friends have no idea that your white friends exist and that you drink domestic beers while playing poker with them every Monday. Your white friends may not know what a fish fry[18] is, let alone that you had one on Sunday with your black friends over SoCo and lime shots. Your life is a delicate balance of pruning Facebook pictures and managing your appointments so as to be all things to most people. Relax and mix it up. While it might feel like ripping off a Band-Aid at first, there is nothing more fun than inviting everyone in your social circles to the same circle and marveling at the fact that people of all races know the lyrics to "Juicy" by Biggie. Just as your friends can integrate, so too can the active parts of your psyche!

D = OPRAH CONSCIOUSNESS

If your primary trait is D, you have reached Oprah Consciousness, which means that like Oprah you are rooted in but not limited to your blackness. You have no internal conflict over eating fried chicken while watching *Jeopardy!*, or getting as excited about *The Goonies* as you do *Coming to America*. Essentially, you are just being yourself without having too many ties to one racial identity over the other. My

---

[18] Unless you're in the South, where fish fries are the only means by which to consume fish.

deepest apologies, for life can be a tad discouraging for you. Because you don't fit into the boxes mainstream culture has designated for you, you will have fewer celebrities to look up to and will, instead, have to lean on alternative methods for fostering self-esteem such as "following your heart," "believing in yourself," and finding friends who "like you for you." You may be baffled by most things marketed to black people, like menthol cigarettes and the McRib, yet also annoyed that there are few people in the culture who look like you associated with things you are interested in. You are an authentic human being on the road to self-actualization, which totally sucks. On the positive, you may be able to transmute your frustration creatively by way of a blog, book, talk show, or independent movie based on your unique point of view.

BLACK MYTH BUSTERS
Affirmative Action

Affirmative Action has often come under attack by mediocre white college applicants worried about hypothetical black applicants taking their positions at their parents' favorite universities. In fact, a lawsuit filed on behalf of one Abigail Fisher who claimed she was denied acceptance to the University of Texas because she is white made it all the way to the Supreme Court in 2013—which is odd, because although it's true that since it was signed into law in 1961 Affirmative Action has helped blacks and other people routinely discriminated against find employment, white women have actually benefited from it disproportionately.

And thank goodness! There was a time when women and black men alike were considered property in this country. Women of all races still face a barrage of beliefs that limit opportunities, as well as blatant discrimination in the workplace. If admissions directors and employers want to give them an extra point as they mull over a sweepingly broad range of criteria, it is really the least such institutions can do. Actually, not trying to dismantle Affirmative Action would be the very least people could do.

As evidenced by Sandra Bullock motivating a giant black man to play football in *The Blind Side*, and Emma Stone encouraging a black maid to leave her only source of income in the midst of the Jim Crow South in *The Help*, white women can be very helpful to the plight of our people ~~according to white Hollywood executives~~. But to be clear, African Americans still earn on average 35 percent less than their white counterparts in the workplace and the median wealth of black households is still twenty times less than that of white ones. So here's hoping one of the white women getting all the jobs will do something about that soon. #Hillary2016

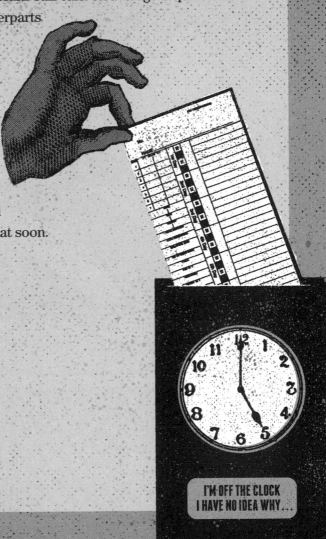

I'M OFF THE CLOCK
I HAVE NO IDEA WHY...

So You've Decided to "Go Black" and Not Come Back

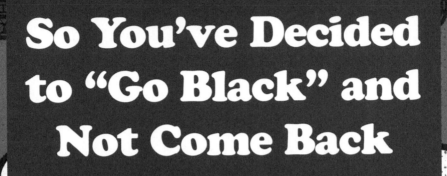

OR, WHY THERE IS SELF-TANNER *AND* SUNBLOCK IN YOUR MEDICINE CABINET

So you've decided to enter into an interracial romance. Congratulations. You're about to take a leap across a chasm of cultural differences in pursuit of a special someone whose presence in your life, you suspect, will bring about the kind of psychological and spiritual growth for which you've been yearning. If, however, your decision to leap across the aforementioned culture chasm is more about how you look strolling through Harlem or rebelling against your parents, leave black people alone. You may have feelings for your new Nubian prince or princess, but you're likely more interested in wearing them on your arm like you would a handbag. Work on yourself. Nobody wants to be your fetish.

More likely, however, the stranglehold that jungle fever can often take over a person's senses is based on the same mysterious and mostly subconscious childhood wounds and neuroses that precipitate any healthy relationship. Mazel.

While your vanilla-chocolate swirl of love will encounter the normal difficulties inherent in any relationship, it will also have the added challenge of bucking whatever preconceived perceptions people have of you.

Black Americans, particularly those who live, work, and/or are educated in multiracial environments, are probably already primed for this experience. Black people who toggle between different racial spheres are always keenly aware of their race. Whether overtipping a white waiter to challenge his perceptions of black patrons or being mistakenly shown to the R&B section in a hipster vinyl shop, they are constantly on guard against the potential negative and positive assumptions other people may have about them.

However, for a white person dating their first black person, that wave of self-consciousness that washes over them when they go to hold their sweetheart's hand at a mostly black family reunion or a Kevin Hart movie might be a brand-new experience. So let's walk through some common concerns.

Being a White Face in a Black Place

Most black people are used to the feeling of being the only black person at an event or party, explaining the plot of *Boomerang* to fascinated white people. When they go with their white lover to meet friends at the beach, the rooftop of a downtown loft, or one of those outdoor decks with Christmas lights inexplicably hanging everywhere, it probably won't be their first time in mostly white company. For white people, however, the experience of being the only one in the room who doesn't know the melody to "Black Happy Birthday" by Stevie Wonder can be new. Relax.

If this feeling of anxiety describes you when the song "Niggas in Paris" comes on and everybody but you starts to recite the lyrics, take solace. This is how your black partner always feels outside the safety net of family and close friends. What a tremendous bonding opportunity this presents you!

For black folks dipping their toes in Lake Vanilla for the first time, it would be wise to recognize that the uncomfortable feeling that over-comes you when you're being forced by your partner to watch reruns of *How I Met Your Mother* might be felt by your Caucasian counter-part for the first time when he or she is traveling in your primarily black sphere. The good news here is that forcing your partner to suffer through things that mostly interest you is a pastime as old as love itself, and can often lead to wonderful new discoveries. Interracial mating is a source of innumerable treasures in our society, such as Lisa Bonet. It also allows older people of different racial groups to come together for the first time and pretend to tolerate each other for the sake of their coupled children. It's through interracial relationships that white peo-ple's eyes are opened with regard to microaggressions and how black people discover that Mayer Hawthorne is not whatever Motown-era soul artist they've been pretending to recognize.

Race Trader or Traitor?

Despite all its benefits, interracial dating does have its opponents. Depending on what part of the country your Oreo cookie of love is formed in, one or both partners in an interracial relationship may come under fire from the people around them. In liberal commu-nities, a white person bringing a black lover over for dinner can be met with a near suspicious amount of fawning and congratulating. However, this is not always the case. Bigots have historically used everything from political power to the Bible to stop people of different races from being together. And though most of them are currently using the Bible and political power to unfairly keep gay people from getting married, bigots are like cockroaches. You may not always see them, but they're there somewhere, waiting to ruin your love life and vote for a Tea Party candidate.

Conversely, both members of an interracial couple can sometimes come under fire within black communities. White people in interracial relationships are sometimes accused of taking all the good black men or women, with their lover of color taking heat for going "outside the race." Black people, like most people of color in this country, have had to fight hard to maintain an independent sense of identity, which makes this a sensitive and controversial subject. As far as your dear author is concerned, this falls into a bucket labeled "your problem, not mine." It's people's prerogative to decide for themselves not to date anyone outside of their race, but to blame others for not living by the same rules feels a bit counterproductive. Take personal responsibility for your own choices in life, let that newfound sense of self-acceptance take hold, and get some cute new selfies up on your BlackPeopleMeet account! Your Nubian prince or princess awaits!

Why's There Coconut Butter in the Bathroom?

When sleepovers between lovers turn into cohabitation, there is often a level of shock and intrigue. A woman discovers it's Rogaine keeping her man's head of hair so full, and a man learns it's a box of chemicals keeping his woman's red head from going gray. It's also when interracial couples discover a bevy of products they never knew existed. Yes, you may have to explain to your black boyfriend that white people need both suntan and sunblock lotions depending on the season. Yes, you may have to explain to your white girlfriend that coconut butter is not an exotic new transfat-free cooking oil from Whole Foods; it's the thing keeping your skin from ashing up like a cigar. These little cultural exchanges are normal, and a part of getting to know each other. Try not to let on how confounded you are at the sight of a do-rag.

Jungle Fever and Other Things You Shouldn't Watch Together

Jungle Fever is an excellent movie, but it will end your interracial relationship upon watching it. You will be convinced that dating a person of another race will somehow get you addicted to crack. Steer clear of this as well as other racially divisive experiences such as going to a Sarah Silverman comedy show or discussing the O. J. Simpson case. Over time, your love will not only bloom but take root, allowing you to endure some of the examples above. But to keep your swirl from melting too soon, it's better to play it safe at the start and avoid the aforementioned.

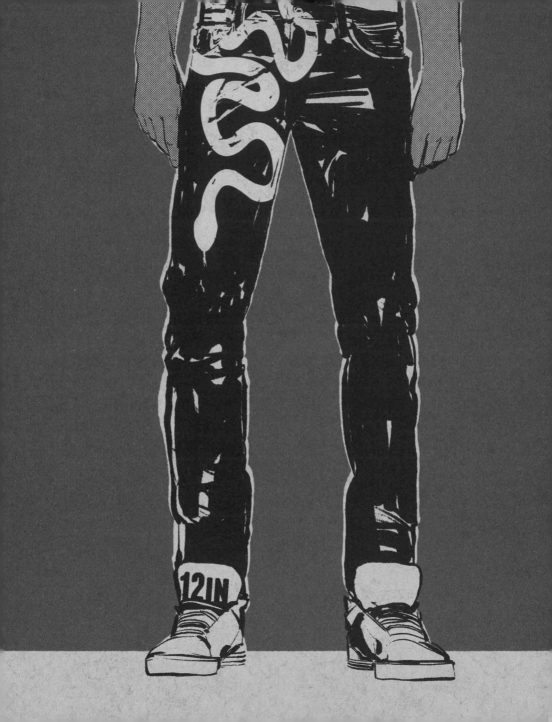

BLACK MYTH BUSTERS
Giant Penises

Thanks to rap music and society's tendency to exoticize people of color, the myth of the giant black dick has endured for some time. Once used as a tactic to discourage interracial sex (the effectiveness of which has long since been overturned in the era of Kim Kardashian), this myth has been seen by some as a "positive stereotype."

While most black men would never go on record to say this, the stereotype can lead to a number of awkward postcoital conversations and explanations. Though this stereotype might be helpful in the wooing stages of romantic courtship, there are few things less sexy than a man having to explain why his black dick isn't as big as his lover hoped it would be. Not that I would know, of course. Your dear author has only the positive stereotypical qualities associated with black people. I'm writing this while dribbling a basketball at a national hip-hop dance/sports competition I plan on winning before running for president of the United States and dropping a surprise album with Jay-Z.

The truth is, the average dick length and width is the same for all men regardless of ethnic background. In spite of the sometimes helpful wide-angle lens on the iPhone used in dickpic-ing, most guys are packing between five and seven inches. And, no, porn stars of any race are not a good barometer of "average."

Why You Can't Have a Dear Black People or a White History Month

OR, THE CHAPTER ABOUT REVERSE RACISM

Why is it that this book, in some instances, can get away with a blanket statement about white people and not be racist, but that when a white person makes a negative blanket statement about a group of black people, it *is* racist? When a black person says that white people "can't dance" or that they really need to "stop Insta-gramming their hikes," aren't they stereotyping all white people? Isn't dedicating a whole month to the achievements of black peo-ple a form of making one group more special than the other? Why is it okay for black students to have a Black Student Union, but white ones can't? Why do the black kids sit together at the school cafeteria? Why can't there be a *Dear Black People*? Isn't all this exclusivity and enforced privilege a form of . . . reverse racism?

Yes! And it's as close to slavery reparations as black folks are likely to get, so *BAM!* Obamacare forever!

Relax, I am kidding. In some ways it depends on your definition of racism. Racism for some people can simply mean the expres-sion of a thought about another race that offends someone of that race. In essence, prejudice. But racism, the kind that people out-side the mainstream culture experience, is more than prejudice. Prejudice against black people is backed up by power. That power, though sometimes wielded subtly, results in a disparity of opportunities between white people and people of color in this country. It isn't prejudice against blacks alone that causes housing discrimination, or that prompts banks to treat loan applicants differently depending on their race. It's not just a couple of black jokes that keep black workers from making as much as their white counterparts, or accounts for the gap of self-esteem between white children and children of color, which can be attributed to images in the media. No. It's prejudice plus power that creates racism. The negative ideas about people of color are baked into a system set up, intentionally or not, to keep them at a disadvantage.

It is tempting to point to the dictionary's definition of racism, which sometimes gives the impression that racism and prejudice are interchangeable, but David T. Wellman dedicated more than a few dictionary lines to defining racism in his book *Portraits of White Racism.* In it he essentially defines racism as a system of advantages based upon race. Dr. Beverly Daniel Tatum, in her book *Why Are All the Black Kids Sitting Together in the Cafeteria? and Other Conversations About Race,* elucidates further by saying "like other forms of oppression, [racism] is not only a personal ideology based on racial prejudice, but a system involving cultural messages and institutional policies and practices as well as the beliefs and actions of individuals. In the context of the United States, this system clearly operates to the advantage of whites and to the disadvantage of people of color." The fact that most dictionaries in defining racism stop short at noting that it only affects groups of people not in power, is further evidence of how racism operates in this country.

Making a crack like "Dear White People, Stop Trying to Make Me a Vegan" doesn't feed a system that stops a white person from getting a job. It doesn't affect a white person's access to healthcare or education, or financial tools such as a bank loan. A white person cracking jokes about black stereotypes does feed such a system, because that system already exists as a disadvantage to blacks and thrives upon these negative attitudes. The worst thing this book will do is make a select few feel butthurt. At best it will validate the feelings of people of color and enlighten white people to the experiences of the other.

To wrap things up and to answer the questions that began this admittedly solemn chapter: There is no need for a White History Month, because the whole of American culture and society already does a thorough job of congratulating white historical figures for their contributions to society, which inadvertently makes children who aren't white feel they have no place in it. A White Student Union at a predominately white school is unnecessary because, essentially, the majority of the school is already one big White Student Union. The black kids get to sit together in the cafeteria without being racists for the same reason all the jocks, cheerleaders, band kids, and basically all the other white kids at the school get to sit together. Finally, a *Dear Black People* would not only be racist, it would be redundant. It's impossible to be black in this country and not be constantly bombarded by the subtle messages and presumptions placed upon us by white people in positions of power.

For those wondering where the "joke" is in this particular chapter, my apologies. In order to maintain the appearance that this book is primarily meant for entertainment purposes, so as to covertly lull you into thinking critically, I will provide the following joke that opens a list of jokes on the popular website racist-jokes.info:

What's yellow and black and makes you laugh? A busful of niggers going over a cliff.

Funny, right?

Glossary of Terms

According to my white friend, and expert on black slang, Spencer Gilbert

The following is a list of words—some used in this text and some not making the rounds in circles of black people and, by default, Jewish comedians. This list is meant to expound on terms in the book as well as help decipher pop music for listeners of all races! As slang tends to be updated and/or abandoned the moment it reaches critical mass, none of this is likely to be accurate by the time this book goes to print.

5-0: (n.) Police officer; taken from the popular 1970s police procedural *Hawaii 5-0*.
"Honey, my brooch is missing. Don't let the maid leave; I'm calling 5-0."

100: (adj.) The genuine article, the real deal. Typically used in the phrase "keep(ing) it 100."
"This rave has bottomless molly water? They truly are keeping it 100."

Bae: (n.) Affectionate term denoting one's primary relationship partner.

"What are you up to this weekend?" "Bae and I got an adorable cabin in Tahoe for our anniversary."

Becky: (n.) A blow job. Named as such due to white girls' (with names like Becky) perceived expertise in oral sex.

"The way she wraps her lips around the straw in that chai latte makes me think she'd give spectacular Becky."

Black Twitter: (n.) A phenomenon that describes the prevalence of afrocentric topics that begin to trend on Twitter once white users finish watching *The Voice* and go to bed.

"Black Twitter destroyed Sam Rubin for confusing Samuel L. Jackson with Laurence Fishburne!"

Bruh: (n.) Informal form of "brother," meaning friend or confidant. Also a phrase white people sometimes use to endear themselves to black people they just met.

"Good looking out on that stock tip last week, my bruh bruh."

Cop: (v.) To purchase or otherwise acquire.

"Be right over, gotta stop at the farmers' market first. I'm finna cop some of that organic watercress."

Dime: (n.) A woman of great beauty, scoring a 10 out of a possible 10 in attractiveness.

"Say what you will about Rachel Maddow, but I think Hillary Clinton is an absolute dime."

Dro: (n.) Potent marijuana that has been produced with the aid of a hydroponic growing system.

"I convinced my doctor to give me a dro card for my gluten sensitivity."

Dope: (adj.) Stylish, hip. Less commonly used to refer to marijuana or heroin.

"J.Crew makes the dopest capri pants, but Old Navy's are the cheapest."

Fam: (n.) Term of affection toward someone in one's own peer group; informal shortening of "family."

"Greetings, fam; I'll have the almond macchiato as usual."

FOH: Abbreviation for "fuck outta here." Can be used to express disgust or disbelief.

"FOH with that epidural; I told you I want a natural birth!"

Fuckboi: (n.) Pejorative term for someone lacking in courage and/or fortitude.

"Trent really threw me under the bus during the marketing presentation. He can be such a fuckboi sometimes!"

Hater: (n.) Someone who is negatively disposed toward you without sufficient cause, likely due to jealousy.

"I just went halfsies on a timeshare. Bye-bye, haters."

Holla: (v.) To greet or get in touch with. Can also mean "flirt with" or "seduce" in a romantic context.

"You'll be at the Malibu ashram for Labor Day too? Holla at your girl!"

Kicks: (n.) Men's shoes, usually sneakers.

"A well-maintained pair of Sperry Top-Siders are the freshest kicks a man can own."

L: (n.) A loss or failure, as opposed to a W, meaning "win."

"This brunch buffet is extremely subpar; let's just take the L and go hiking."

Lean: (n.) Codeine cough syrup. If imbibed in large enough quantities, serves as a source of intoxication and inspiration for southern hip-hop artists.

"My cough still won't go away, even with the lean Dr. Nusbaum prescribed."

Microaggression: (n.) An act of covert oppression, usually in the form of a well-meaning comment that nevertheless accentuates the "otherness" of its receiver due to a stereotype.

"I know it's meant to be a compliment, but being told I look like Diana Ross because I'm wearing eyeliner really feels like a microaggression."

Main chick: (n.) Girlfriend, as opposed to your "side piece," or mistress.

"I only take my side piece to the gastropub; my main chick gets tapas."

Plug: (n.) A purveyor of highly specialized, often illegal goods.

"My acupuncturist hooked me up with this extravagant ginger liniment; he's definitely the plug."

Ratchet: (adj.) Describes an aspirational person, place, or thing that nonetheless lacks in class or social grace.

"Red wine with halibut? If that's not ratchet, I don't know what is."

Read: (v.) The act of lowering another's self-esteem via a brutally honest assessment of their appearance, personality, etc.

"You don't like The Daily Show? *Stand back, I'm about to read this bitch."*

Shade: (n.) Indirect or otherwise subtle disrespect toward another.

"Did you forget to wash your lacrosse jersey? Because coach has been throwing shade at you all practice."

SMDH: Acronym for "shake my damn head." Indicates contempt and/or disappointment. Most commonly seen on Black Twitter.

"I'm pretty sure they didn't even decant this cabernet, SMDH."

Swag: (n./adj.) Short for "swagger." Presenting oneself with extreme confidence and style.

"Brendan got promoted to associate manager and now his swag is out of this world!"

Swerve: (v.) An exclamation that signals your intent to avoid an unpleasant person or situation.

"Would you mind dog-sitting Bark Ruffalo while Kevin and I are on vaycay?" "Swerve."

THOT: (n.) An acronym for "that ho over there." A promiscuous woman of little consequence.

"I see you and Susan are getting pretty serious, do I hear wedding bells?" "Of course not, Preston; she's just another THOT."

Trap, the: (n.) A den of ill repute. Typically where drugs are sold.

"Honey, I can hear Steven in the background. You're still in the trap, aren't you?" "I told you I had to work late!"

Trill: (adj.) Exceptionally authentic. A portmanteau of "true" and "real."

"There were two crème brûlée food trucks at the art walk, but only the vegan one was trill."

Turnt: (v./adj.) The state of being (or process of becoming) cheerfully inebriated.

"Make sure you tell all the junior staff not to get too turnt at the Christmas party."

Whip: (n.) An automobile.

"The lease is up on my whip. I've got my eye on that new Subaru Forester."

Yay: (n.) Cocaine. Also known as "yak," "yayo," or "white girl."

"I haven't seen this much yay since the Princeton-Yale reunion game."

YOLO: (n.) Acronym for "You only live once" as popularized by the Drake song "The Motto."

"They say it's getting more dangerous to go backpacking across Europe, but then again, YOLO."

Acknowledgments

I'D LIKE TO now acknowledge a few folks in my life, without whom this book would be terrible. Or more terrible, depending on how the experience of reading it went for you.

My friend and platonic life partner, Lena Waithe, for being a near-incessant, always encouraging supporter of every iteration of *Dear White People*, as well as telling me, over pancakes at Kitchen 24, "you know our steps are divinely ordered," every time something bad happened along the way. Also for helping refine my intellectual justifications for loving *The Wiz* by having the opposite opinion.

My publisher and editor, Dawn Davis, whose generous laughter at our initial meeting calmed my nerves and somehow convinced me that a) anyone would want to read a book I'd written, and that b) my string of consciousness ramblings would work as a book.

Thanks also to my Simon & Schuster production team, especially Dana Sloan, Navorn Johnson, Kimberly Goldstein, and Kristen Lemire.

To this book's illustrator, Ian O'Phelan, for brilliantly employing both his design and side eye.

To my beautiful, sweet, intelligent, warm, caring mother, who has always been my number one fan.

To the supporters of every race of *Dear White People*, who've let me know that my work has meant something to them. You validate my purpose in life. Thank you.

My friends and producing partners whom I began the *Dear White People* journey with. Ann Le, for always asking questions that force my point of view outside of whatever box I've confined it too. Angel Lopez, for always being able to speak to the heart of the matter. And to Lena Waithe . . . I already acknowledged you, don't get greedy. #TheWizForever

My friends and producing partners whom I've continued the *Dear White People* journey with. Stephanie Allain, for giving me the best advice ever when dealing with adversity, which was "Give yourself thirty minutes to be sad, then move on. We got work to do!" And to Effie T. Brown, for her tenacity and can-do energy, without which I would have fewer gray hairs.

My friend and producer Julie Lebedev, who in every way made the culmination of the *Dear White People* journey possible.

Oprah Winfrey, whom I'd like to acknowledge in a blatant attempt to get to meet her. Also because, cumulatively, her programming and life mission have surely added up to more self-confidence for me and openess to the possibilities of the universe than I'd otherwise have. Seriously though, call me.

My WME family, especially my literary agent, Jay Mandel, and my agent agent, Charles King, for having my back and spotting talent in me from the very beginning.

My manager, Ben Rowe, for all the support and great ideas, as well as David Lonner, for his support and vision.

My lawyer, Gordon Bobb, the very first person in Hollywood to sign me, without whom I'd sign any and everything, no questions asked, because legal copy frightens me.

My assistant and friend Anthony Williams, for your boundless enthusiasm, brilliant observations, and your uncanny ability to both deal with the levels of hot messery of which I'm capable and to clean it up.

Cameron Washington, for being a bright source of inspiration, for introducing me to Nichiren Buddhism, and for always being willing to do the Beyoncé body roll from Michelle Williams's "When Jesus Say Yes" video at almost a moment's notice.

Baratunde Thurston, who, despite writing a better book than me, encouraged me to publish mine anyway.

And finally for anyone who's ever disagreed with me and thus forced me to either know why I stand for what I stand for or to be open to learning something new.

About the Author
and the Illustrator

JUSTIN SIMIEN is the writer and director of the critically acclaimed feature *Dear White People*, which won the Special Jury Award for Breakthrough Talent at the Sundance Film Festival in 2014. Simien was also featured in *Variety* magazine as one of 10 Directors to Watch. Justin gained national attention after making a "concept trailer" for his then unproduced screenplay of *Dear White People*, which went viral on YouTube, garnering over a million views and fifty thousand dollars in donations from around the world. He has contributed to CNN.com and The Huffington Post.

IAN O'PHELAN hails from Toledo, Ohio. He is a graduate of the University of Cincinnati, where he studied fine art and graphic design. His work has been shown in galleries in Detroit, London, Los Angeles, and New York.